Text: Arturo Martín Mac Kay Fulle
Photographs: Ignacio Cateriano Rostworowski

Copyright © Roberto Gheller Doig

Schell 319 of. 803 Miraflores Lima-Peru Telephone: (51-1) 994140037

e-mail: gheller.ra@pucp.edu.pe

First Edition: July 2011 / **Second Edition:** February 2013

Original Title / Título Original: Perú. País de Leyenda

Text: Arturo Martín Mac Kay Fulle

Editor: Roberto Gheller Doig

Graphic Design: Elizabeth Albarracín V.

Map: José Manuel Mamani

Translation: Stephen Light (www.eltraductoringles.com)

Photographers: All the photographs are by **Ignacio Cateriano Rostworowski** except those on the following pages: a= Above, b= Bottom, c= Center, r= Right, l= Left. Mario Sánchez Proaño: 16(a,l), 119(a,r); Jorge Esquiroz: 69, 140, 141; José Enrique Galera: 137(a,r); Federico Kauffmann Doig: 118(b,l); Sothebys: 61(b,r), 61(b,l); Yutaka Yoshii: 3, 16(b,r), 16(b,c), 16(b,l), 17(b,l), 30(a,l), 30(b,r), 30(b,c), 30(b,l), 31(a,r), 30(b,l), 30(b,c),38(b,r), 39(a,r), 60, 61(a,r), 61(a,l), 72(b,r),72(b,l), 72(b,c), 73(a,l), 75(b,r), 112, 113(a,l), 113(b), 118(a,l), 118(b,c), 118(b,r), 128(b,l), 131(a,r), 131(b), 132(a,l), 132(a,r), 132(c,l), 136(a,r); Joaquín Rubio: 17(a,l), 17(a,r), 17(b,r), 36, 38(a), 38(b,l), 38(b,c), 73(a,l), 73(a,c),74(a,l), 75(b,l), 75(b,c), 113(a,c), 113(a,r), 119(a,c), 128(a,l), 128(b,r); Alejandro Balaguer / PromPerú: 52(b,l), 88, 96(a,r); Mylene D`Auriol / PromPerú: 08, 89; Manchamanteles / PromPerú: 12(b,l); Renzo Tasso / PromPerú: 52(a,l), 53(a,r); PromPerú / PromPerú: 68(a,l); Carlos Sala / PromPerú: 79(a,l); Renzo Giraldo / PromPerú: 79(b); Giham Tubbeh / PromPerú: 97, 137(b); Michael Tweddle / PromPerú: 100(a), 100(b,l); Carlos Ibarra / PromPerú: 100(b,r), 101(a,l); Wilfredo Loayza/ PromPerú: 101(a,r); Heinz Plenge / PromPerú: 104(r,c), 130(b); Josip Curich / PromPerú: 106; Enrique Castro Mendívil /PromPerú: 107(a), 107 (b,l); Cecilia Larrabure / PromPerú: 108(b,r); Renzo Uccelli / PromPerú: 111; César Vega / PromPerú: 115; Aníbal Solimano / PromPerú: 110, 114, 136(b,r); Walter Silvera / PromPerú: 116, 122(b); Daniel Silva / PromPerú: 124(b); Domingo Garibaldi / PromPerú: 134; Gonzalo Barandiarán /PromPerú: 136(a,l); Pilar Olivares / PromPerú: 136(b,l); Walter Hupiu / PromPerú: 137(a,l); Beatrice Velarde / PromPerú: 139; Luis Yupanqui / PromPerú: 138

Printing: Printed in Peru by Le Crayone de Nancy Margarita Salazar Trujillo. Calle C- Mz. C- Lt. 2A- Urb. Los Pinos de Monterrico - Lima 33

Copies: 1000

Hecho el depósito legal en la Biblioteca Nacional del Perú

N°: 2013-00483

ISBN N°: 978-612-46187-8-9

Contents

Acknowledgments
The editor expresses his gratitude to the following individuals and institutions for their collaboration in this publication:

- Walter Alva Alva
- Andrés Álvarez Calderón
- Rosa Amano
- Fray Ernesto Chambi Cruz
- Banco Central de Reserva del Perú
- Banco de Crédito del Perú
- Compañía de Jesús
- Régulo Franco Jordán
- Lourdes Grupp de Arias
- Hacienda Mamacona
- Hoteles Casa Andina
- Inkaterra Asociación
- Federico Kauffmann Doig
- Fernando López Mazzotti
- Stephen Light
- Luis Martínez Vargas Torrico
- Héctor Méndez Fachín
- P. Oscar Morelli Müller S.J.
- Museo Amano
- Museo de Arqueología de la Universidad Nacional de Trujillo
- Museo Rafael Larco Herrera
- Promociones Turísticas del Sur S.A.
- Proyecto Arqueológico El Brujo
- Diego Rizo Patrón
- P. José Enrique Rodríguez S.J.
- Gustavo Siles Doig
- Museo Tumbas Reales de Sipán
- Proyecto Arqueológico Huacas del Sol y de la Luna
- Juan Julio Rosales Olano
- PromPerú
- Juan Carlos Yankelevich
- Yutaka Yoshii
- Patricia Vega Gutiérrez

Peru.

Peru. Strategically located in the central zone of South America, Peru is the third largest country in the region, after Brazil and Argentina. Its rich biological diversity, characterized by a great variety of ecosystems, has made it one of the most important focuses of concern for those who seek to conserve the world's natural heritage.

However, it is Peru's history and culture that make it a unique territory, a land the cultural expression of which emerged from the fusion of a plurality of identities and idiosyncrasies.

The presence of humankind in Peru dates back to 10 000 BC, but it was around 3000 BC when the founda-

tions of what would become the great Andean civilization made their first appearance. The monumental architecture of Caral reflects the early existence of complex societies with highly developed economic, political, religious and social systems. It was the mastery of agriculture in the valleys of the arid coast and freezing mountains that formed the ba-

■ **Above:** Fiesta of "Mamacha Carmen" in Paucartambo, Cusco. **Right:** Peru's diverse regions and microclimates produce a wide variety of fruits and vegetables throughout the year, forming the basis of a varied cuisine.

The Peruvian handcraft tradition is one of the most diverse and appreciated in the world.

The *marinera* dance, Peruvian Paso horses and gastronomy can be enjoyed at Hacienda Mamacona, situated next to the Pachacamac archaeological complex.

sis for the emergence 1500 years later across the territory of the Andes of the great ceremonial centers, the corollary of which would be Chavín de Huántar.

Around two thousand years ago, new regional groups emerged. On the northern coast the Moche culture appeared, renowned for its metalwork and pottery; in the south Paracas developed, with its textiles, funerary bundles and advances in medicine; and shortly afterwards came Nasca, with its marvelous lines and figures traced onto the desert. Towards the end of the 6th century, the El Niño phenomenon wreaked havoc on the environment and, therefore, upon existing political structures, leading to new cultural expressions of an imperialistic character. In this context, Wari culture arose in the southern highlands, followed by Sicán on the northern coast, and these cultures encouraged the mass production and distribution of their textiles and pottery as a method for spreading their power and ideology.

Sometime around the 12th century, new regional states made their appearance in ancient Peru. the northern coast was dominated by Chimú, and on the southern coast the Chincha culture developed, with its great maritime and overland trade networks. In parallel, in the highland and forest regions, the Cajamarca and Chachapoyas cultures formed warrior kingdoms that controlled vast territories.

Finally, in the 14th century, emerging from the Cusco valley, the Incas initiated a period of expansion that would culminate with the creation of the largest empire ever seen in pre-Hispanic America; the territory of Tawantinsuyu would eventually stretch as far as present-day southwestern Colombia and northwestern Argentina. Like the Roman Empire, the dominance of the Incas was based upon a bureaucratic state system, through which they created a system of roads and agriculture with which they managed to overcome the vertical geography of the Andes.

In 1532, Francisco Pizarrro launched the Spanish conquest and, split also by an internal crisis, Tawantinsuyu came to an end just two years later, giving way to the most significant center of Spanish rule in the Americas, the viceroyalty of Peru.

Between the 16th and 19th centuries, Lima and its port, Callao, formed the core of the political, economic and cultural life of Peru. The colonial era was the melting pot in which the contributions of every immigrant group were merged. Arabs from the Spanish Levant and the Maghreb, blacks from Western Africa and, after independence, Chinese from Canton and Macau, Japanese from Okinawa, Germans and Austrians from the Tyrol and Italians from Liguria, gave Peru its mixed and syncretic identity.

Our gastronomy reflects that miscegenation; ceviches and beverages take us back to the Moche and Incas, stews and soups recall our Spanish heritage, rice and stir-fry dishes call to mind the influence of Asia, candies speak to us of the Moors who arrived with the conquistadores, and sausages and pastas remind us of those who came from Europe in search of a better future.

In Peruvian folklore, traditional festivities enable us to travel back in time through the colorful dances of Cusco, Puno and Ayacucho, taking us back to the glory of the pre-Hispanic past, while the dances of the coast —such as the classic mari-

■ Through its modern design, the Larco Museum displays a complete archaeological collection presenting the development of pre-Hispanic culture in Peru.

■ Many Peruvian dishes benefit from the flavors of different types of chili pepper.

Pucará bulls, symbols of prosperity, are an example of syncretism.

Stir-fried beef is a fusion of Peruvian and Chinese traditions.

In Peru's interior, people continue to wear bright traditional clothing that survives as a reminder of a past in which textile art was a medium for cultural expression.

nera— recall the pomp and grandeur of the viceroyalty. In processions in honor of Catholic saints, the Christianity brought from Europe is fused with Andean traditions.

Of Andalusian origin, bullfighting and cockfighting also form an essential part of these festivities, and they are practiced still in Lima and the other large coastal cities, as well as in the remotest regions of the highlands. The Peruvian Paso horse, that pride of our national heritage, is descended from Arabic steeds, bred for galloping easily over the endless sands of the coast.

■ Very close to Lima it is possible to enjoy an exhibition of Peruvian Paso horses presented at the Hacienda Mamacona.

With the advent of the Republic, those first decades of freedom were very difficult. Civil wars, external wars, economic crises and coups d'état took the fledgling country to the brink of chaos. In the midst of such political and economic uncertainty, the formative process that was forging Peruvian identity and its unique expressions continued to be enriched by the contributions of new blood from all over the world.

Presidents including Ramón Castilla and José Balta gave the black slaves their freedom, broke with the servitude of indigenous people and encouraged the immigration of Europeans and Asians.

These new communities formed part of the nation and even fought to defend it in its most tragic hour, when in 1879 the conflict with Chile that would come to be known as the War of the Pacific began. The war would last for five years and bring disastrous consequences for Peru.

The second half of the 1880s until 1919 was a period of national reconstruction. The first civilian governments were established, industry was developed and the earliest concepts of democracy and equality emerged. The country was changing and integrating its various components. During the middle of the 20th century, Augusto B. Leguía and

Luis Miguel Sánchez Cerro became the first men of mixed race to assume the presidency. A significant boost to indigenous culture came during a brief interval in the democratic process, between 1968 and 1979, when the state itself adopted a series of measures, such as the granting of official status to the Quechua language.

Peru is the fruit of those thousands of years of development. Our history is a journey characterized by successes and failures, during which many diverse experiences and traditions came together to give form to the multicolored and multicultural country we now offer to the world.

City of Kings.
After the conquest of the Inca Empire, Francisco Pizarro established his capital in a strategic zone, close to water sources and very near the ocean. On January 18 1535 he founded the City of Kings in the Rímac Valley, and over time it became known by its indigenous name, Limac,

and was transformed into the political, economic and cultural heart of the viceroyalty of Peru and much of Spanish America. But this city was not only the hub of Spanish power in the central Andes; as it developed it also became a great melting pot, with its heterogeneous population of native-born Americans, Europeans, Africans and Asians creating a new, idiosyncratic culture. Today, Lima is a city with a thoroughly hybrid base that is characterized by great social and geographic contrasts; in a few minutes one can go from emerging neighborhoods to modern business and residential districts, or leave the shores of the Pacific Ocean for the foothills of the Andes.

■ **Above:** Balcony of Archbishop's Palace. **Right:** Main portico of Lima's cathedral. Two great bell towers built in the 18th century lend the structure the neoclassical style associated with the Spanish Bourbons.

Chancay ceramic depicting two musicians carrying panpipes and a drum.

Lima Culture As a contemporary of the Nasca and Moche civilizations (100 – 800 AD), the Lima culture developed in the valleys of Chancay, Chillón, Rímac and Lurín, where a stratified society composed of fishermen, farmers and ceramists flourished, led by lords who governed from enormous pyramids and temples. The distinctive characteristic of the Lima culture was its spectacular architecture. They built pyramidal structures using small rectangular mud bricks arranged upright like books on a shelf, including the administrative complexes of Maranga, Pucllana and part of Cajamarquilla. These structures were decorated with beautiful polychrome friezes representing their principal deities.

Chancay Culture Between 1000 AD and 1300 AD, the Chancay culture developed from the fertile lands of the valley of the same name to the arid bay of Ancón. Characterized by its milky white ceramics decorated with black paint and its attractive textiles, Chancay established a series of chiefdoms which disseminated their art through maritime and overland trade routes.

Textile Art Together with those of Paracas culture, Chancay weavers are considered among the best of ancient Peru and their production of painted mantles and enormous gauzes was outstanding. In spite of their fineness, these weavings have been conserved thanks to the arid-

Magical-religious dolls from the Chancay culture.

Lima ceramic decorated with a two-headed serpent surrounded by chili peppers.

Chancay ceramic: individual with headdress, ear ornamentation and ceremonial cup.

Chancay textile: The cloth was used like a canvas, upon which birds, fish, mythological being and geometric forms were painted.

Textile painted with zoomorphic decoration featuring reptiles and a school of fish.

ity of the desert and their impeccable structural technique.

Wooden and Clay Sculpture The Chancay people enabled us to learn about their way of life and even see what they looked like through their art in wood and clay. Their craftspeople depicted the faces of ordinary people and the elite, as well as details of their clothing, headdresses and even their tattoos. Classic examples of this type of artistic expression can be seen among the famous *cuchimilcos*.

Classic *cuchimilco*, the most representative form of Chancay pottery.

Kelim tapestry decorated with seabirds, lizards and monkeys.

■ View of the circular plaza and Main Pyramid of the sacred city of Caral, one of the first organized settlements in pre-Hispanic Peru and the prototype for cities on the American continent.

■ Depiction of daily life at Huaca Pucllana.

Caral: the earliest civilization Situated 180 kilometers north of Lima, in the Supe Valley, and dating back some 5000 years, Caral is a great religious and administrative complex composed of monumental pyramids, circular plazas, altars and residential areas, revealing the level of political, economic and religious organization achieved. Together with Egypt, Mesopotamia and India, Caral is one of the original centers of the birth of world civilization. In 2009 it was declared a World Heritage Site by UNESCO.

Huaca Pucllana This mud brick building, located in the modern residential district of Miraflores, was one of the largest constructions of the height of Lima culture, around 500 AD. Its pyramidal structure fulfilled both administrative and religious functions, and important offerings have been found, including pottery, the remains of foodstuffs and human sacrifices. After it was abandoned, the shrine continued to be respected as an important sacred site, particularly by the Wari, who used the pyramid as a burial site.

Pachacamac, the Delphi of the Andes

Located in the lower part of the Lurín Valley, the earliest structures at Pachacamac date from the Lima period, and the site continued to be used until the time of the Spanish conquest. It was the Ychsma who spread the worship of Pachacamac, their principal deity, who was the creator of all things and the force that animated all living creatures. The fame of its oracle attracted thousands of pilgrims who came in search of solutions to their problems and answers to their questions, and in their gratitude they offered tribute and gifts. The Spanish chroniclers tell of the importance of this cult, which continued into colonial times, merged with the sacred image of the Christ of Pachacamilla, or the Lord of Miracles.

Plaza Mayor

The Plaza Mayor symbolizes the importance of Lima as the seat of Spanish power in South America and, subsequently, of the Republic of Peru. The most important and beautiful buildings around the plaza display a blend of artistic and architectural

■ *Acllahuasi* at the Pachacamac Archaeological Complex.

■ Changing of the guard at the Government Palace.

■ Lima's Plaza Mayor, surrounded by colonial-style buildings, with their broad carved wooden balconies and Moorish-style porticos.

Central nave of Lima's cathedral with its vaulted ceiling, the sober neoclassical style of which contrasts with the baroque style of its altarpieces.

styles ranging from the 17th century to the 20th century. The Government Palace (House of Pizarro), the Municipal Palace, the Casa del Oidor, the Archbishop's Palace and the Cathedral stand as fine examples of this conglomeration of emblematic buildings.

The Cathedral The original cathedral (1540) was quite modest, but in 1636 the first major construction was completed, in an effort to raise it to the same level as its counterpart in Seville. During the 1746 earthquake, part of the structure collapsed, and so the viceroy Antonio Manso de Velasco ordered the construction of a new church. Towards the end of

The baroque-style Chapel of Our Lady of the Evangelization.

the 18th century the towers it possesses today were added. The cathedral is now home to a religious art museum in which paintings, furniture and a number of 17th century liturgical objects are displayed.

Basilica and Convent of San Francisco

With the founding of Lima the Franciscan order was granted a piece of land. In spite of the renovation work made necessary by the earthquakes that have devastated the capital, the predominant style remains baroque, with Moorish influence. This church and convent houses canvases from the Flemish school of Peter Paul Rubens, together with a number of gold and silver objects, as well

■ Library of the convent of San Francisco, where a spectacular collection of books and manuscripts dating back to the 15th century is conserved.

■ View of the vaulted architecture of the "catacombs" situated beneath the church of San Francisco, where high-ranking members of colonial-era society were interred.

■ Church of San Francisco, an example of Spanish Lima's baroque architecture.

■ Façade of Torre Tagle palace, now the foreign ministry building. Its stone and stucco portico is complemented by elegant balconies.

■ Moorish-style balconies of Casa de Osambela, a mansion dating from the 18th century.

as a sacristy carved from hardy cedar, the colorful paintings of Francisco de Zurbarán and José de Ribera, the library and crypts, or "catacombs", which served as a burial place for members of guilds and brotherhoods.

Church of San Pedro Constructed in 1569 by Jesuit priests, San Pedro dis-

plays a combination of renaissance, Plateresque, baroque, Churrigueresque and neoclassical styles. The main altar is adorned with the images of Saint Peter and Saint Paul and the image of the Sacred Heart of Jesus. Another important feature is the Altar of Relics, a beautiful renaissance style altarpiece which holds several relics of the Holy

Martyrs. All of these elements combine to make San Pedro the most famous church in Lima's historic center.

Palacio de Torre Tagle Constructed in 1735 by the Marquis de Torre Tagle, today this is the seat of the Foreign Ministry and one of the most beautiful and best preserved buildings in the

■ **Left:** Interior of the San Pedro basilica, one of the most beautiful churches in Lima, with its baroque decoration adorned with gold leaf, Seville tiles and Moorish-style motifs.

■ View of Plaza San Martín, built in 1921. At its center stands an equestrian statue of the liberator of Peru, General José de San Martín, sculpted by the Spanish artist Mariano Benilure.

■ The Magic Water Circuit is one of Lima's more modern attractions.

capital. It is remarkable for its stone portal in the baroque style, balconies, colonnades and Moorish-style doors, and its interior architecture with Churrigueresque flourishes including Seville tiles, elements that combine to transport us back to the splendor of 18th century Lima.

Plaza San Martín Built as part of the celebrations to mark the centenary of national independence,

Plaza San Martín is —after Plaza Mayor— the most important public space in Lima. At the center stands the equestrian statue of the liberator José de San Martín, surrounded by Art Nouveau buildings typical of the European modernism of the beginning of the 20th century. Teatro Colón, Hotel Bolívar and Jirón de la Unión were the de *rigueur* meeting places of the Lima society of the time.

■ *La Rosa Náutica*, a beautiful and emblematic European-style restaurant, enhances the magnificent Pacific coastline of the capital. It is popular with tourists and Lima's business, political and social elite.

Miraflores A district of Lima since the mid-19th century, is one of the most attractive parts of modern Lima, and it brings together the major commercial and business centers, modern apartment buildings and many parks and beaches that serve as meeting places for local inhabitants and visitors. Miraflores is the Lima of the future, while at the same time conserving the traditions of the erstwhile Garden City.

■ *Bajada Balta* and *Puente Villena* in the commercial and residential district of Miraflores.

■ Viewing point at the modern Larcomar shopping mall in Miraflores.

■ Medalla Milagrosa church at Parque Kennedy, in Miraflores.

■ The *Parque del Amor* is one of the most emblematic attractions in the city, where couples and newlyweds come to have their photograph taken or just to enjoy the view.

■ The main square in Barranco, surrounded by neoclassical buildings.

Miraflores Parque Kennedy, or Parque Central Created to commemorate the US president John F. Kennedy, this 20,000 square meter park is the focus of the business and social life of Miraflores. Here, artistic shows are presented, typical Lima snacks and sweets are enjoyed, and antiquarians and painters offer their work for sale. The Palacio Municipal and the beautiful Virgen de la Medalla Milagrosa church overlook the park.

Barranco This bohemian district was the preferred bathing resort of Lima society in the 19th century, until it was destroyed during the War of the Pacific. After its reconstruction, it became the haunt of artists and intellectuals, which has lent a special character to its streets, colonial and republican style houses, many parks and its traditional Puente de los Suspiros ["Bridge of Sighs"].

Right: Puente de los Suspiros ["Bridge of Sighs"], evoked by the composer Chabuca Grande, is Barranco's iconic attraction. The bohemian atmosphere of this district makes it popular with locals and tourists. ■

Life in the desert. A few hours south of Lima, in a setting where the ocean's waves crash against beaches that stretch away to form infinite deserts, the traveler comes to Paracas, small in size and population but big in terms of resources and attractions. Its name comes from the Quechua word *paraca*,

which is the name for the strong winds loaded with sand that are typical of the arid lands of the south of the country, and which shaped the lives of the ancient inhabitants of pre-Hispanic times. Today, Paracas is a popular tourist destination thanks to its wide deserts, beautiful beaches rich in marine fauna, cultural attractions and protected natural areas where it is possible to observe the seabirds, fish and mammals of what is a unique ecosystem. For the comfort of its visitors, Paracas is also blessed with one of Peru's most modern and complete hotel infrastructures, and people come to enjoy water sports, nature and culture, or relax.

■ **Above:** Pair of Inca terns (*Larosterna inca*). **Right:** Peru's southern coast is an enormous desert whipped by strong winds; the *"paracas"* that shape the enormous sand dunes among which great cultures like Paracas emerged.

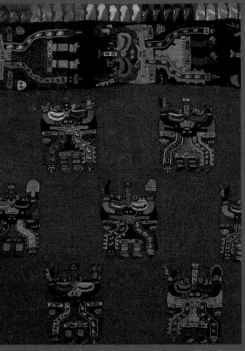

Embroidered Paracas Necropolis phase mantle.

Paracas Culture In 1925, Julio C. Tello began his excavations at Arena Blanca and Cerro Colorado, on the Paracas peninsula, where he discovered extensive cemeteries. At these sites he recovered many funerary bundles, and through his excavations and subsequent analysis of the bundles, he proposed the existence of two cultural phases.

Paracas Caverns In this first stage, the Paracas culture buried its dead in tombs dug in a form resembling "an inverted glass". Each tomb contained several bundles, and the bodies were wrapped with plain cloth, as well as being accompanied by double-spout and bridge-handled vessels, and brightly-colored bowls decorated with incised motifs and painted in red, yellow, brown, black and white after having been fired in kilns. Pieces painted using the negative resist technique were also produced during this period.

Paracas Necropolis In the next stage, the Paracas culture buried its dead in large semi-subterranean structures, divided into several chambers in which the funerary bundles were placed. The bodies were wrapped in elegantly embroidered textiles featuring an elaborate iconography expressed in vibrant colors. These were the large mantles (up to 1.30 meters long) that had first attracted Tello to the Paracas area. The bodies were arranged in baskets in a sitting position with their knees bent, and they were wrapped with several layers of plain cloth which alternated with more elaborate textiles, gold ornaments and headdresses made from the feathers of tropical birds.

Paracas Necropolis phase ceramic modeled into the shape of a gourd.

Anthropomorphic Paracas Caverns phase vessel with painted and incised decoration.

Pottery representation of a Paracas fisherman with nets and fish.

Paracas Weavers: art and color The Paracas people became highly-skilled in the technique of embroidery and the combining of colors, as well as the use of three-dimensional textiles, with which they decorated the borders of the mantles. Experts consider the textiles of the Paracas Necropolis phase the most beautiful produced in pre-Columbian times. In mantles made from cotton and camelid fiber, they embroidered anthropomorphic figures as well as aspects of local flora and fauna. Some researchers have speculated that the transformations and rites depicted in these beautiful works may be related to the concept of fertility and the agricultural calendar.

Skull Deformation Another characteristic aspect of Paracas culture was the custom of skull deformation. From a very young age, children's heads were bandaged and wrapped in splints which caused the shape of the skull to be altered as it developed. It is thought that in this way kinship ties to different social or ethnic groups could be identified.

Skull Trepanning Excavation work at Paracas cemeteries has provided important information regarding this culture's advances in medicine, their main achievement being skull trepanning. Through these operations, they would extract the fractured part of a skull and replace it with gold or silver plates. For such procedures they employed obsidian knives, while the imbibing of alcoholic beverages such as *chicha* served as a method of anesthesia.

In Paracas mantles each embroidered element of the design is unique.

Paracas culture skull deformation may have served to identify this people.

Paracas skull with several orifices attributed to trepanning.

Funerary bundle from the Paracas Necropolis phase (watercolor by Pedro Rojas Ponce).

The fertile seas off Ica wash against the desert shore, eroding the cliffs and creating scenic rock formations. The sea played an indispensable role in the birth, evolution and success of Paracas and, later, Nasca culture.

Flocks of seagulls soar over the islets situated close to the coastline of Paracas.

Paracas National Reserve The exceptional biological diversity of the Paracas National Reserve is produced by the Humboldt current and coastal upwelling, which places these seas among the most fertile and productive in the world. It is possible to find 216 species of birds, more than 180 species of fish and 20 species of cetaceans in these waters, including seabirds, flamingoes (*Phoenicopterus chilensis*), Humboldt penguins (*Spheniscus humboldti*), seals and sea otters, as well as dolphins and whales.

This protected natural area is also renowned for its beautiful beaches of reddish sand, which combined with the winds typical of the area and its warm climate make Paracas an excellent setting for adventure sports. The reserve is also an important historical site, for it is home to a number of Paracas culture archaeological re-

■ Flamingos take a break from their migratory journey on the beaches of Paracas. According to popular tradition, these birds inspired the red and white bands of Peru's national flag.

■ Geoglyph known as "El Candelabro", the origin of which remains a mystery.

■ The territory of Paracas regales the visitor with fascinating rock formations shaped by the ocean.

mains and it was here, in 1820, that the liberation forces of General José de San Martín disembarked. In 1991, the reserve was declared a Ramsar site by the Convention on Wetlands of International Importance.

Ballestas Islands Located off the coast of the Paracas peninsula, the Ballestas islands are an archipelago composed of half a dozen small, rocky islets inhabited by thousands

■ The Huacachina oasis provides a delightful contrast with the dunes that surround it.

■ "La Maternidad" is the part of the Ballestas Islands where female seals care for their young, which are 80 centimeters long and weigh up to 15 kilograms at birth.

of South American sea lions (*Otaria flavescens*) and millions of seabirds, including Guanay cormorants (*Phalacrocorax boungainvillii*), Inca terns (*Larosterna inca*) and the Peruvian booby (*Sula variegata*). There is no permanent human population, but it is possible to see part of the installations employed in the extraction of guano, which was used during the 19th century as a fertilizer for the barren soils of Europe and North America.

Above: One of the most emblematic species of the Paracas National Reserve is the Humboldt penguin, which is adapted to the conditions of Peru's southern coast. **Right:** South American sea lion (*Otaria flavescens*); the male can weigh up to 300 kilograms. ■

Enigma of the desert.
In one of the most arid regions not only in Peru, but in all of South America, one finds the city of Nasca. The area is famous throughout the world for its beautiful ancient ceramics, trophy heads and, above all, for its enigmatic lines traced upon the desert's surface.

But Nasca offers more than a glorious and mythical past; its people have conquered an arid and hostile territory in order to develop abundant harvests of dates, pecans, grapes and Lima beans, all of which find their way to the tables of ordinary homes throughout Peru, in products ranging from subtle candies like its famous "*chocotejas*", to fine pisco, Peru's national drink. To all this is added Nasca's success as an attraction for adventure sports enthusiasts. Today, in the deserts of Nasca the sands are used for sand boarding or racing dune buggies, activities which enable visitors to experience the harsh beauty of this arid land.

Above: Pictorial Nasca ceramic. **Right:** For agricultural societies, control of water sources is essential, and it is believed that the Nasca Lines were ritual pathways associated with the mountains, which were seen as divine water sources.

Nasca Culture

Pottery The Nasca people are renowned for their beautiful polychrome pottery, which employed as many as twelve tonalities, was carefully polished and made with thin walls. Their designs included both sacred and secular imagery, as well as abstract and naturalistic motifs, ranging from easily identifiable symbols to the Anthropomorphic Mythical Being. The most common form for these vessels was the bridge-handle and double-spout bottle. Other typical items produced using clay included their panpipes and drums.

Textile Art In common with their Paracas predecessors, the Nasca people were skilled weavers. They combined cotton and wool, favoring dark crimson, yellow and turquoise, and they decorated their textiles with geometric designs, flowers and the ubiquitous trophy heads.

Trophy Heads The warriors who participated in ritual combat decapitated the prisoners they took and conserved their heads, which were carefully prepared. The base of the skull was broken and stretched, and the eyes and brain were removed. The forehead was perforated and a rope was passed through the hole and used to hang the trophy head. Finally, the lips were sealed with one or two cactus thorns. These trophy heads

■ Bottle painted with the typical Nasca culture mythological being.

■ Pictorial ceramic with naturalistic decoration.

■ Ceramic decorated with trophy heads.

■ Trophy heads were a symbol of power among the warrior elite.

The Cantalloc aqueducts were built by the Nasca people to irrigate the arid land of the valleys they occupied.

Nasca weaving embroidered with feathers in the shape of trophy heads.

are found in groups, suggesting that their taking, preparation and burial were considered necessary for the regeneration and continued growth of plants. This theory proposed by Daniel Proulx is supported by graphic representations of fruit emerging from the mouths of trophy heads.

Nasca Lines One of the most remarkable achievements of Nasca culture is the series of geoglyphs located on the plains and slopes of the Rio Grande river basin, which can only be seen from the air. There exist two types: the geometric forms (trapezoids, triangles, zigzags and straight lines that continue for many kilometers); and the biomorphic images (gigantic naturalistic creatures: birds, monkey, spider and killer whale) that cover several hectares.

They were constructed using a very simple technique: the small, dark stones on the surface of the desert were removed, exposing the underlying sand. However, the mathematical

A 49-meter geoglyph of a dog.

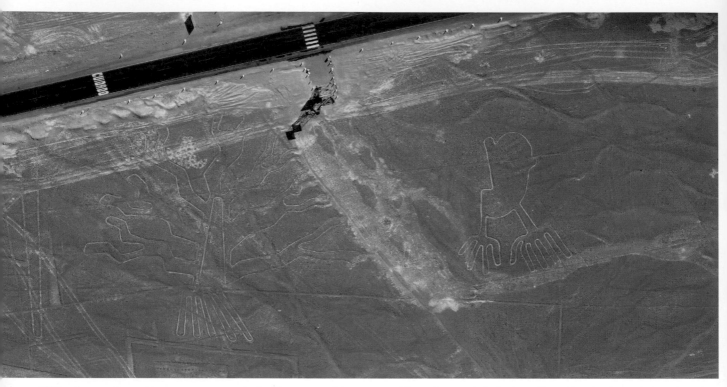

■ The famous Nasca Lines are composed of anthropomorphic, zoomorphic and geometric designs. From the viewing point on the edge of the highway the tree, hands and lizard figures can be seen.

■ Geoglyph of the condor, which dominates the skies of the Andes.

and technical aspects involved in their design are extraordinary, such as the tracing of such long and yet perfectly straight lines, as well as the intricate arcs and geometric figures, not to mention the difficulties involved in producing such large figures. We know that they were made by the Nasca people because the same designs are present in their iconography, although the geoglyphs of Palpa and Llipata more closely resemble Paracas designs than those on the Ingenio plain, known collectively as "the Nasca Lines".

There has been much discussion and speculation regarding their purpose. Recent archaeological work has uncovered several offerings associated with the geoglyphs, including the remains of mollusks, fish

■ A nine-fingered monkey with a long, playful tail shaped like a spiral is an example of fauna not seen on the Peruvian coast.

■ The spider, symbol of fertility for ancient Peruvians.

■ The flamingo, a migratory bird with a large beak and long neck, is represented by one of the biggest images etched into the Pampas del Ingenio. It is 300 meters long and its beak points east.

■ The geoglyphs traced onto the desert sands were created by the Nasca culture and their Paracas predecessors, who also illustrated their world view with designs like this one situated at Llipata and known as "La Familia".

and ceramics, indicating that they may have been linked to rituals designed to ensure the supply of water.

Cahuachi Cahuachi was the center of political and religious power, and it was composed of a series of pyramids and plazas covering an area of 24 square kilometers. It is located 42 kilometers from the sea and 18 kilometers from the city of Nasca.

Archaeological research has shown that over time the ceremonies performed at the tops of the pyramids were restricted to the elite, while popular ceremonies were held in the plazas. Music formed an indispensable part of these ceremonies, as indicated by the large number of panpipes and drums found at the site, as well as the frequent depiction of musicians in the iconography of Nasca ceramics.

Right: The Great Pyramid forms part of the administrative, political and religious center of Cahuachi, the most important Nasca culture ■ site and the hub of an extensive zone of ideological influence that incorporated neighboring valleys.

Lava, sky and stone.

Founded on the banks of the Chili River by the conquistador Garci Manuel de Carbajal in 1540, Arequipa is Peru's second city in terms of size and political and economic importance. Inca Huayna Capac conquered the region occupied by the chiefdoms of Churajón and Chuquibamba.

During the viceroyalty, Villa de la Asunción de Nuestra Señora del Valle Hermoso was transformed into the economic hub of southern Peru by virtue of its mining and agricultural resources and its textile industry, while both the city and the region were well-known for their loyalty to the Spanish crown. Later, after independence, Arequipa was transformed into the setting for insurrections, like those launched in 1950 and 1955 against the government of Manuel A. Odría.

The White City —a reference to the color of *sillar*, the volcanic stone common to the region with which chur-

■ **Right:** Arequipa's neoclassical style, gothic-influenced cathedral, built from *sillar*, stands on the northern side of the Plaza de Armas. Its façade is decorated with seventy classical style columns, three doorways and two side arches. It has two renaissance-style towers.

■ Arequipa cathedral's main altar, made from Carrara marble.

■ Three-tiered Plaza de Armas fountain crowned by an archangel; nicknamed Tuturutu by local people, it has been a silent witness to riots, protests and celebrations.

ches like La Compañía and convents like Santa Catalina were built— is known for its beautiful scenery and climate; enormous snow-capped volcanoes rise above a fertile countryside which supports an important agricultural sector.

The Plaza de Armas and Cathedral Arequipa's Plaza de Armas and cathedral have been recognized by UNESCO as World Heritage Sites. The cathedral was built between 1540 and 1656 with *sillar* and is decorated with Carrara marble and woodcarvings imported from France. As a result of the earthquakes that have occurred over the centuries, the cathedral has undergone extensive restoration and enlargement, and its architecture and decoration exhibit a number of styles, ranging from baroque to gothic and neoclassical. The centerpiece of the Plaza de Armas is its beautiful bronze fountain, and the square is surrounded by attractive portals behind which are located the city's most important public buildings, dating from the viceroyalty and republican periods. These include the old jail, the royal treasury and the city hall. Today, these portals harbor stores, businesses and restaurants frequented by locals and visitors. The fountain in the middle of the square is decorated with the sculpture affectionately known as the Tuturutu, a goblin according to some, or the city's guardian angel according to others.

■ Dining room of Casa del Moral, with period furniture.

■ Doorway of Casa Tristán del Pozo, also known as Casa Ugarteche or Ricketts, which dates from the early 18th century. It is one of the finest examples of the Andean baroque style in *sillar*.

■ Main inner patio of Casa Tristán del Pozo.

The Mansions Built from *sillar* during the 18th century, the city's great mansions typify Arequipa-style architecture. Conceived in the Andean baroque style, these houses possess unique characteristics, such as the portals decorated with stone carved into classical-style pillars crowned with the coats-of-arms of the

Façade of Compañía de Jesús church: It has two floors and its rich decoration constitutes the finest example of the Andean baroque style in Arequipa.

Detail of the façade of Compañía de Jesús church.

house's owner. Another characteristic is the use of entrance halls and large rooms with vaulted ceilings. The city's most important mansions [or "*casonas*"] include Goyeneche, Tristán del Pozo, del Moral, del Maestre Bustamante, Irriberry and Casa de los Pastor.

Church of La Compañía Located between Portal de la Municipalidad and Portal de las Flores, this church was built between 1590 and 1698 by the Jesuit Order. Like all the city's great buildings, this baroque-style church was constructed using sillar. It is remarkable for its Andean baroque façade, murals and frescos, as well as the paintings it houses by the Italian artist Bernardo Bitti.

Church of Santo Domingo This church belongs to the Dominican Order, which erected the first church in 1544. The construction we see today was begun ninety years later and is one of the finest examples of indigenous baroque architecture. The ornamentation of the *sillar* walls, composed of vines and roses, cherubs and angels, is admired by all those who visit this old church.

Church of San Francisco Famous for its library and art gallery, which date from the 16th century, San Francisco distinguishes itself from the other churches in the center of Arequipa with its baroque structure, which combines stone, brick and *sillar* in what is an expression of Indian, Spanish and creole influences.

■ Detail of the arches and columns of the Compañía de Jesús cloister.

■ In the cloisters of Compañía de Jesús arches and columns combine in perfect harmony as a testament to the inexhaustible imagination of their architects.

■ The Los Naranjos cloister dates from 1738 and is decorated with oil paintings and murals.

■ Calle Córdova, decorated with plant pots sown with red geraniums.

■ The Santa Catalina convent is a microcosm of the architecture produced in Arequipa from the 17th to the 19th centuries.

Convent of Santa Catalina Built at the end of the 16th century by the order of Saint Catherine of Siena, this convent covers an area of 20,000 square meters composed of fascinating narrow streets, archways and *sillar* cupolas. Two of the most characteristic elements of indigenous baroque art, the paintings of the Cusco School and great carved wooden altars, make this silent and magical place one of the most remarkable attractions of the White City. Since 1970 the public has been allowed to visit the convent, the original architecture of which is embellished with beautiful reddish tones and flowers that add their own contribution to the harmony of the place.

Right: Plaza Zocodover: Its name comes from the Arabic word "zoco", which means "barter". On Sundays the nuns would gather here ■ to trade the embroidery, weavings and other products they made.

■ Fertile countryside of Arequipa with El Misti volcano in the background.

■ The frozen body of "Juanita"; the girl was about 14 years-old when she died.

■ Main patio of the mansion where the "Santuarios de Altura" museum houses the remains of the mummy "Juanita", together with the offerings she was buried with.

The *Capacochas* and the Mummy "Juanita" One of the most important rituals of the Inca Empire was the *capacocha*, one of the manifestations of which involved the selection of children from society's elite, who after the performing of certain rites were sacrificed and left as offerings at the summits of the snow-capped mountains of the Andes. At the summit of Mount Ampato, in the Arequipa region, in 1995 the American anthropologist Johan Reinhard discovered one of the best examples of these *capacochas*, or high altitude sanctuaries: the perfectly preserved body of "Juanita", a girl aged about fourteen, who was buried with gold and *Spondylus* figurines, evidence of this complex Inca ritual that apparently sought to integrate the different local elites with the nobility of Cusco and with the Inca deities, through the sacrifice of a child of noble blood, thereby forging an eternal bond between the lineages of regional rulers and the royal governors of the imperial capital.

■ The church of San Juan Bautista is located in the traditional and picturesque Yanahuara district. Its austere interior contrasts with its baroque façade.

■ View from the Yanahuara vantage point. El Misti volcano can be seen in the background.

Colca Canyon, the realm of the condor

Situated between 3000 and 5000 meters above sea level, in the province of Caylloma, northeast of the city of Arequipa, Colca Canyon has a long history and appears to have been frozen in time. It was first inhabited by the Collagua and Cabana ethnic groups, who were conquered subsequently by the Incas. In the 16th century Franciscan missions were established in the area, as well as mining operations for the extraction of silver, particularly around the present-day village of Coporaque. Today, Colca is an important travel destination, not only because of the vestiges of its pre-Hispanic and colonial past found there —particularly its colonial-era churches, which are a living example of Andean baroque— but also because of its considerable biodiversity, with more than 300 species of flora and fauna, as well as geysers and thermal waters.

Recent surveying and mapping work in the area has established that this

■ The slopes of "The Valley of Marvels", as the Nobel Laureate Mario Vargas Llosa calls the Colca Valley, are covered with approximately six thousand hectares of agricultural terraces.

■ The majestic Andean condor, sacred bird of the Incas.

Above: Camelid herding is one of the region's main activities. **Right:** The agricultural terracing carved from the slopes of Colca Canyon ■ date from pre-Hispanic times. The Cabana and Collagua people still sow their crops on these terraces.

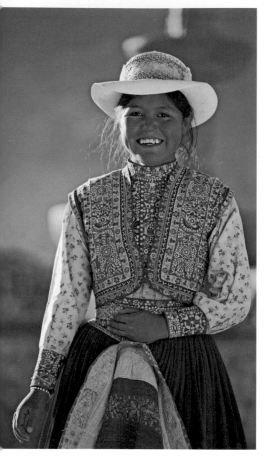

A Collagua woman dressed in an embroidered waistcoat and skirt.

In Maca, the Santa Ana de Miraflores church is one of the finest examples of Andean baroque art. Its altars are richly decorated in gold leaf.

canyon is one of the deepest in the world, with a maximum depth of 3,250 meters. Also, one of its peaks, Mount Mismi, has been identified as the source of the Amazon River.

Above: In Yanque, the church is remarkable for its *sillar* façade decorated with floral and religious motifs. **Right:** A Cabana woman with a bird of prey and embroidered clothing. The shape of their hats is one of the details which differentiate Cabana and Collagua women.

Fiesta on the sacred lake.

At almost 4000 meters above sea level, Puno is the folkloric capital of Peru and the home of more than 300 typical dances which recall a pre-Hispanic and colonial-era past comparable to that of the imperial city of Cusco. Its inhabitants, the Aymara people, are

closely bound to their unique environment, which is dominated by Lake Titicaca, the highest navigable lake in the world, from where, according to legend, the children of the sun god emerged to found the empire of the Incas.

This highland area was the cradle of important cultures such as Pucara and Tiwanaku, and from 1668, when it was founded by the Spanish, Puno became an essential part of the silver route linking the mines of Potosí with Lima and the port of Callao. Today, Puno is still an important commercial zone, where typical products from the highlands and the rest of this southern region arrive before being distributed to other cities throughout Peru.

■ **Above:** Taquile islanders. **Right:** View of Lake Umayo and the *chullpas* of Sillustani, built from carved stone and mud. Both the Colla and Inca people considered this a sacred site worthy of being the final resting place of their ancestors.

Stone sculpture produced by the Pucara culture.

Classic Pucara ceramic, with incised and polychrome painted decoration.

Pucara Culture Pucara culture developed in the northern part of the Lake Titicaca basin from the end of the Middle Formative period and reached its peak during the Late Formative period (from approximately 500 BC to 400 AD). The largest and most important site —considered the "capital" by some experts— is Pukara, and it covers an area of more than one square kilometer and is divided into two general areas: a central area with monumental characteristics where the Qalasaya complex is located, together with the surrounding pyramids and the central esplanade; and the peripheral area near the river, where the residential constructions were located and a large garbage dump existed.

The Domestication of Camelids and High Plains Agriculture Pucara culture was characterized by the breeding and use of alpacas and llamas. These animals provided a mode of transport, meat and wool, contributing to the Pucara people's survival in a hostile climate and terrain. In addition, they began to grow crops around Lake Titicaca, employing raised areas or artificial ridges separated by floodable areas which enabled them to plant in areas where the nighttime frost would normally destroy crops. This farming technique, known in Quechua as *waru waru*, was used in the highlands throughout the entire pre-Hispanic period and can even be seen today.

Tiwanaku Culture After coexisting with the Pucara and other groups, Tiwanaku society managed to dominate an extensive and inhospitable geographic area through its colonization of a number of ecosystems. Through the production of a range of goods and their subsequent trade they established a state that would dominate the region from 400 AD to 1000 AD. A second key to the power of Tiwanaku was the diffusion of their ideology, based on veneration of the so-called Staff God, whose image is depicted on the Sun Gate, a great carved monolith upon which this divinity appears accompanied by winged creatures.

Tiwanaku, architects of the highlands Tiwanaku architecture is characterized by the use of immense blocks of stone that were transformed into spectacular edifices, most of which were pyramidal

■ The Sun Gate, with the image of the god Wiracocha accompanied by his acolytes, is a magnificent example of the religious architecture of Tiwanaku, in Bolivia.

■ The Ponce Monolith: Situated in the urban center of Tiwanaku, Bolivia.

with sunken patios. Tiwanaku, the capital of this culture, covered an area of almost 40 hectares and was composed of religious structures at its core and dwellings and workshops in the outlying areas. The most important structures are the Akapana mound, the Sunken Temple, the Kalasasaya platform and the Sun Gate. The other nearby sites of secondary importance are Lukurmata, Pajchiri and Khonko Wankhane.

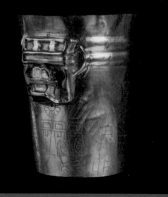

■ Gold *kero*, a typical Tiwanaku ceremonial cup.

■ Wooden *kero* representing a mythological being with feline features.

■ Aymara man steering his reed boat.

■ Women from one of the Uros islands, with their multicolored clothing contrasting with the yellow totora reed from which their islands are made.

Lake Titicaca, the sacred lake Lake Titicaca is set majestically on the high plains. It is the highest lake in the world and the second largest in South America. It is home to an extensive national reserve in which local flora and fauna are protected, and the entire lake area is of great cultural significance, for on its shores and islands visitors have an opportunity to observe both its present and the vestiges of its glorious past.

Islands of Titicaca The lake is dotted with several islands and archipelagos, many of which are inhabited. The ethnic Uru or Kotsuña are remarkable for the construction of artificial totora reed islands, and the spectacular textile tradition inherited from their ancient forebears. These islands vary in size, according to the needs of the families that live on them; usually each island is in-habited by between three and ten families. Homes consist of a single room, and cooking is done in the open air. Some of the structures are roofed with corrugated iron, particularly the schoolhouses and church. A hut has been constructed for those visitors who wish to spend the night with the islanders, while solar panels provide light and there is even an internet connection.

Right: Since time immemorial the islanders have developed their mastery of the textile art; the men knit while the women spin thread. ■ Their products are sold to tourists who visit the islands.

■ A typical reed boat on the great highland lake.

■ As well as being used to build islands, boats and houses, *totora* reed is used to produce enormous sculptures admired by tourists.

■ A *totora* reed house with a conical roof.

■ The simplicity of reed constructions, both in terms of their color and form, blends seamlessly with the unique scenery of the high plains and Lake Titicaca.

Amantani Island This is the largest island in Peru, with an area of more than nine square kilometers, and the remains of an Inca temple are conserved there. The island is best known for its inhabitants, who live from the production of textiles and stone carving.

Taquile Island This is the most populated island in Peru, with almost 2000 inhabitants, and in common with Amantani it boasts archaeological remains from the Kolla and Inca cultures, including the funerary structures known as *chullpas*. The name of the island comes from that of the Spanish governor Pedro Gonzales de Taquila. This is perhaps the most well-known of the lake's islands, by virtue of the

■ Dawn over the island of Amantani on Lake Titicaca: In pre-Columbian times, this great lake was associated with sun worship by the Aymara and Quechua people.

■ Titicaca moderates the temperatures of the great Collao plain, facilitating the human settlement of the islands. Local inhabitants are renowned for their industriousness, evidenced by their farming, livestock, fishing and handcraft activities.

■ Typical archway on Taquile Island, from where the immensity of Lake Titicaca, described by some as an inland sea, can be appreciated. Taquile culture is the product of the blending of Quechua traditions with the Spanish influence present since the 16th century.

fame of its extraordinarily skilled weavers, who produce items with beautiful designs and decorative symbols that identify the characteristics of the wearer, including their gender, marital and social status, etc.

Sillustani This is another of Puno's emblematic attractions. This archaeological site established by the Kolla culture is located 34 kilometers northwest of the city of Puno, on the shores of Lake Umayo. Sillustani is famous for its stone funerary structures, known as *chullpas*, typical of the cultures that once dominated these high plains. Kollas, Lupacas and Incas interred their dead at this site.

Fiestas and Folklore Known as the folkloric capital of Peru, Puno boasts more than 300 dances of Quechua and

■ **Left:** Taquile children with their typical clothing, including the headgear which serves to identify them among their peers. **Right:** The funerary towers or *chullpas* of Sillustani.

■ Multicolored costume used for the *"Diablada"*, one of the region's dances.

■ Phallic sculptures at the Temple of Fertility which —like the *chullpas*— combine the divine with the profane and death with fertility.

Aymara origin, including the *pandilla* and the *diablada*, which are performed during the most famous of the region's festivities: the Fiesta of Candelaria. This celebration is held in honor of the Virgin of Candelaria, the patron saint of the city of Puno, during February in the middle of the rainy season —thereby linking the festivities with the earth and fertility— and its influence has spread beyond the highlands of Puno. It is considered the most important religious celebration in Peru after the Lord of the Miracles. Shortly after Candelaria, carnival festivities begin in the city, with all the color and fervor of the earlier celebration, but with a more marked presence of western influences.

Right: During the Candelaria Fiesta hordes of dancers display their impressive costumes, including the *"Morenada"* dancers, who ■ represent the suffering of the black slaves marched to the mines of Potosí during the colonial period.

Navel of the world. The ancient capital of the Incas is an essential destination for all visitors to Peru, not only because of the vestiges it conserves of its rich Inca and colonial heritage, but also because of its palpable spirit. Wandering through its streets one can appreciate the many faces of Cusco —imperial,

colonial, mixed race, rebellious, pagan, Catholic— awaiting those who wish to discover them. Walking through the capital of Tawantinsuyu, one passes megalithic Inca temples and palaces as well as baroque mansions and churches, all of which stand as testaments to its importance as the cultural and political center of pre-Hispanic and colonial Peru. Cusco is also a place of living culture; in its streets artisans create work in clay, wool, wood and metal, employing ancient traditions, and in local markets one can savor fresh bread, soups and typical dishes which are the product of the syncretism of Spanish and indigenous culture in the Peruvian Andes.

Above: Twelve-angled stone in Calle Hatunrumiyoc. **Right:** The Ausangate region of Cusco is located in the heart of the Andes, where high snow-capped peaks rise above crops and grassland.

The Origins The city's origins date back to the 9th century, when the Killke culture settled in the valley, but it was from the 13th century —after its founding as the Inca administrative center— that it began to truly make its mark on Andean history. According to the tradition recorded by Garcilaso de la Vega, the first Inca ruler, Manco Capac, and his wife Mama Ocllo emerged from Lake Titicaca upon the command of the sun god and founded the city close to Huanacaure hill, where the golden staff carried by the Inca was plunged deep into the earth. In another version recorded by a number of chroniclers, the four Ayar brothers, together with their respective wives, emerged from Tambutocco hill in search of a place to occupy and found a new settlement. After an eventful journey, Ayar Manco and the four women founded Cusco and established the royal lineage of the Incas. It was in March 1534 that Francisco Pizarro founded the Spanish city of Cusco we see today, upon the foundations of the indigenous city, giving it the remarkable character it possesses and which now attracts visitors from all over the world.

The Incas After founding their capital, the Incas began their expansion beyond the Cusco valley, culminating around 1450, by which time Inca Pachacutec had transformed his people into an imperial power ruling a territory that covered present-day Peru, Bolivia and Ecuador, northern Chile, northwestern Argentina and the far south of Colombia. In this way the empire of Tawantinsuyu became the largest empire ever seen in the Americas, one that would unite a whole range of cultural expressions and consolidate the Andean civilization which persists to this day.

Sociopolitical and Economic Organization The Inca Empire was a centralized state that recognized the figure of the Inca as both sovereign and god. This ruler resided in the capital, Cusco, entrusting and distributing his power

■ Gold anthropomorphic figurines typically found as Inca offerings.

■ Aryballos were pottery vessels used by the Incas to store liquids.

■ Inca bottle with tubular neck decorated with painted designs depicting *cantuta* flowers.

■ The *kero* or ceremonial cup was adopted by the Incas from other highland cultures.

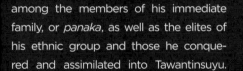

■ A woven wool bag with tassels and fringes, decorated with llama designs.

■ The *quipu* was a mnemonic device for storing information.

among the members of his immediate family, or *panaka*, as well as the elites of his ethnic group and those he conquered and assimilated into Tawantinsuyu.

Nevertheless, it was the extended family, or *ayllu*, which was the most important component of the social and political machinery of the empire. This basic unit was the instrument of organization and control that ensured the smooth running of the Inca state in the central Andes. A chain of command existed in which the head of each family answered to a superior who was in charge of a group of families, and so on, so that the Inca bureaucracy could satisfy their needs and ensure they met their

tax obligations. Reciprocity and redistribution were the twin pillars of the economic structure of the empire.

Through this system, goods and labor were accumulated, so that the surplus produced might serve the entire population; in this way the social bonding and favor were created which united an empire that incorporated thousands of kilometers, hundreds of ethnic groups (many of them subjugated) and millions of inhabitants, including the ordinary people, or *hatun runa*, the vanquished, those who had been transported to other lands, or *mitmaqkunas*, and the servant class, known as *yanaconas*.

To this end, work was organized in different ways, the most important of which was the *mita*, which consisted of the provision of labor to the imperial state. The practice of *minka* involved working for the community or those in need, or laboring on the sacred lands of the sun god, Inti, the official state deity, while *ayni* meant working to help the other members of one's own *ayllu*, or family unit.

These ways of organizing work functioned well thanks to strict and efficient communication between the power hierarchy and the sovereign in Cusco, and this was made possible by a system of

■ Offerings in the form of figurines could be made from gold, copper or *Spondylus*.

■ Wall of the ancient palace of Inca Roca over which the Spanish built a mansion that is now the Archbishop's Palace and Museum of Religious Art.

roads that united all the provinces with the capital. This network was known as the Capac Ñan, or Royal Way, and parts of it can still be seen. The system served as the basis for the modern Peruvian highway system. These roads were used by couriers, known as *chasquis*, who carried important information over great distances, using *tambos* along the route to rest and feed themselves.

The Inca economy was based on agriculture, particularly the cultivation of tubers (mostly potatoes), cereals and corn. They had to produce enough to feed a population of millions, and they achieved this through technical innovation. The Incas devised a number of ways of optimizing work on the land, including the use of terracing, raised fields, aqueducts, natural fertilizers and agricultural laboratories like the one found at Moray in Cusco.

In terms of livestock, they raised camelids as beasts of burden and for their meat and wool. Fishing and hunting were limited to certain territories but the products of such activities could be obtained throughout the empire thanks to the aforementioned infrastructure.

Other important activities in Tawantinsuyu were metalwork in gold, silver and *tumbaga*, an art learned from the people of Peru's northern coast, and textile manufacture using cotton and wool. Inca pottery was characterized by aryballos and the use of the *kero*, both of which served a ritual function associated with libations. Unlike the work of their forebears, Inca pottery was limited to a few forms and the decoration employed was characterized by simple lines and geometric forms.

One of the most notable facets of Inca culture was their mnemonic accounting system, the *quipu*, a device employing knots of different types, positions and colors to record the movements of products and persons, and which also served to record information over time. This system was the responsibility of the *quipucamayocs*, masters who instructed their apprentices in the use of the *quipu*, so that their knowledge was transmitted from generation to generation until the Spanish conquest in 1532.

Inca Religion In common with all the societies that emerged in the central Andes, the Incas' belief system was polytheistic. The Inca sovereign was believed to be descended from the principal deity, the sun god, or Inti, whose main temple was the Qorikancha in Cusco. Through religion, the Incas consolidated their power throughout the empire. Each province paid tribute to Inti, and he was worshiped in small local temples known as *ushnus*.

Below Inti in the pantheon was Wiracocha, the principal deity of the original inhabitants of Cusco, possibly imported from the high plains, or *altiplano*, to the south during the Tiwanaku period. Wiracocha was the most popular god among the population that formed the heart of the empire. Below these two divinities, we find a whole pantheon composed of celestial beings and the forces of nature, such as Quilla (the moon), Pachamama (the earth), Pachacamac (the god of earthquakes) and Illapa (lightning).

The Incas perceived the world as divided into three realms, with the gods inhabiting the world above, or Hanan Pacha, mankind occupying the world of the living, and the ancestors ruling in Uku Pacha, the underworld. All of these spaces were integrated by the figure of the Inca, as the supreme organizer of the universe.

■ Inca pitcher with a face on the neck and painted decoration featuring ferns.

■ *Paccha* type ceramic shaped like a foot plow, or *chaquitaclla*.

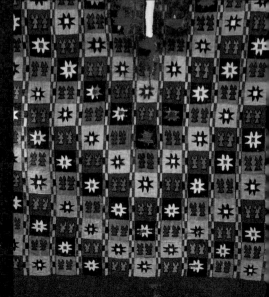

■ *Unku*, or Inca tunic, decorated with a star design.

■ View of the Plaza de Armas, in which the cathedral can be seen to the left and the Jesuit church to the right. The square is surrounded by eight magnificent portals: *Belén, Carrizos, de la Compañía, Comercio, Confituría, Panes, Harinas* and *Carnes.*

Plaza de Armas Known during Inca times as Haucaypata, Cusco's main square is surrounded by old houses and colonial-era arcades, as well as baroque churches erected over the ancient residences of the Incas Viracocha, Pachacutec and Huayna Capac. It was here that the celebrations to mark Inti Raymi ["Festival of the Sun"] were held, and where in 1781 José Gabriel Condorcanqui, or Tupac Amaru II, was executed.

■ Detail of the carved cedar wood baroque-style choir stall created by indigenous artists. Behind the seats the panels are decorated with the images of saints.

■ Main altarpiece of the Sagrada Familia church adjacent to the cathedral.

■ Altar of Forgiveness with a central image of Our Lady of the Nativity located opposite the main door of the cathedral, also known as the Door of Forgiveness.

The Cathedral The construction of the cathedral dates from 1539, and blocks of stone quarried from the ruins of Sacsayhuaman were used to build it, while its foundations rest on what was once the palace of Inca Viracocha. The structure we see today is the result of the remodeling and enlargement finalized in 1664 which gave the cathedral its combination of styles, with baroque and gothic predominating. The finest canvases from the Cusco School and oil paintings brought from Europe between the 16th and 18th centuries line the interior walls of the cathedral.

■ Magnificent carved cedar main altar of the Jesuit church.

■ Chapterhouse of the monastery of Santa Catalina decorated in the 18th century with a theological and moralistic themed mural attributed to Tadeo Escalante.

Church of the Society of Jesus *La Compañía* is the tallest church in Cusco. It was built by the Jesuits in 1668 over what had been the Amarucancha. Narrower than the cathedral, this church is remarkable for its two towers, crowned with the round windows that reveal its massive bells. The atrium and altar rival those of the cathedral and it is one of the finest examples of Andean baroque art.

■ Inca stone walls in the interior of the Convent of Santo Domingo-Qorikancha. According to Garcilaso de la Vega the Incas worshiped sun, lightning and thunder.

The Convent of Santo Domingo was built over the principal Inca temple: Qorikancha. Its architecture displays the superimposition of Spanish elements over Inca walls.

The Reception Room

The main cloister of the Convent of Santo Domingo is surrounded by a series of arches and paintings depicting the life of Saint Dominic de Guzmán, founder of the Dominican Order.

Convent of Santo Domingo – Qorikancha This is the most striking of Cusco's churches. Santo Domingo rises above what was once the Qorikancha, the most important temple for veneration of the sun god and the pantheon of Inca deities during the time of Tawantinsuyu, beginning with the reign of Pachacutec. Construction of the church began in 1663, under the auspices of the Order of Preachers. Its interior features the finest aspects of viceroyalty art and architecture, with Roman arches, classical columns, Cusco School paintings, gold leaf and numerous liturgical objects fashioned from silver.

■ View of Sacsayhuaman in which the zigzagging shape of its walls can be seen. They are said to represent the Inca god of lightning, Illapa.

■ Its colossal walls mean Sacsayhuaman is mistakenly described as a fortress.

Sacsayhuaman Situated to the northwest of Cusco, dominating the heights above the city, Sacsayhuaman is an enormous stone structure composed of three zigzagging parallel walls. According to some experts, this temple was dedicated to the god Illapa, while others believe it was a place for the worship of water. Others claim it was a fortress, given the battles that were fought there after the Spanish invasion and the structure's central role in the rebellion led by Manco Inca. To-

day, the esplanade facing Sacsayhuaman is the setting for the annual Inti Raymi festivities.

Qenko Located very close to Sacsayhuaman, Qenko was undoubtedly a religious site, and it is believed that rites were performed here associated with fertility, given its proximity to underground water sources. The site's "amphitheater" and the stone altar set in a small cave make it a popular attraction.

■ Pucapucara is a structure distributed across three levels composed of walls, terraces, stairways, aqueducts and a plaza. It is believed that it was a *tambo,* or wayside inn, used by the Inca's entourage en route to Tambomachay.

■ Tambomachay is a small Inca site remarkable because of its complex hydraulic system and perfect trapezoidal doorways and windows, which stood as an emblem of the presence of the Inca state in the hills surrounding Cusco.

■ Pisac displays all the perfection characteristic of Inca stonework. Its fine pink granite walls combine with the greenness of the Sacred Valley.

■ Great *huanca* or monolith located in the middle of the amphitheater at Qenko.

Pucapucara Strategically located at the top of a rock outcrop at the eastern access point to the city of Cusco, this archaeological site is known as a fortress, apparently designed to defend the imperial capital. However, its storage structures imply other functions for this "red fortress" (the translation of its Quechua name).

Tambomachay In common with many Inca temples, Tambomachay was a site devoted to the worship of water and fertility, but unlike other sacred places around Cusco, this shrine provides definite evidence of these types of rituals: aqueducts, channels and pools (known as baths) in which the use of water not only demonstrates the Incas' skill in hydraulic engineering and the shaping of the landscape, but also the ideological importance of such activities.

The Sacred Valley - Pisac A little farther from Cusco, more than 30 kilometers to the northeast of the city on the banks of the sacred Vilcanota River, stands the archaeological complex of Pisac, composed of pink granite structures arranged around an Intihuatana,

■ Monolithic pink granite walls of the Temple of the Sun at the Ollantaytambo archaeological complex.

■ The Chinchero church, built like Santo Domingo in Cusco over the foundations of an Inca structure.

or sundial, and extensive agricultural terracing. According to legend, Pisac is the petrified body of a beautiful Inca princess who failed to keep her word and was punished with a terrible curse.

Ollantaytambo This is the largest of the archaeological complexes in the Urubamba valley, composed of a series of structures devoted to the worship of a number of Inca gods, including the sun god, Inti. Visitors can also see some of the finest examples in the whole of Tawantinsuyu of the Incas' impressive hydraulic systems and agricultural terracing. The construction of this impressive place was begun by Inca Pachacutec and it became the occasional residence of his successors. After the conquest it was transformed into a stronghold of the resistance led by Manco Inca, before he was defeated and forced to withdraw to the forests of Vilcabamba.

Chinchero Together with Qorikancha, Chinchero is another example of the cultural syncretism that developed after the Spanish invasion in the 16th century. The erstwhile palace of Inca Tupac Yupanqui was used as the base of the beautiful baroque church built in 1607. The church houses an impressive series of murals and serves as the focus of a local handcraft fair and market, as well as pro-

■ Moray was an experimental agricultural center where the Incas sowed crops at different altitudes. The circular terraces set at different levels made it possible to reproduce up to twenty microclimates.

viding an excellent viewing point from which to contemplate the surrounding landscape, including Mount Verónica. Chinchero also attracts visitors because the villagers are skilled weavers, and their woolen products are highly-prized by Peruvian and foreign tourists alike.

Maras and Moray Maras is famous for its salt pans, which as well as providing an important economic activity for local people also offer a fantastic visual attraction for visitors, who can observe more than 3000 pools filled with white salt that contrasts with the dark brown surface of the mountain. Some 5 kilometers away is Moray, an Inca agricultural laboratory composed of a series of concentric terraces which replicate a number of microclimates. Here, Inca specialists were able to investigate the relationships between different products and variations in humidity, altitude and solar radiation. In this way they were able to optimize the productivity of species grown in different parts of the empire.

■ Salt pans in the village of Maras, composed of some 3000 pools.

■ A fountain forming part of the Inca hydraulic system at Tipón.

The Southern Valley - Tipón To the south of the Sacred Valley, near the village of Oropesa, is Tipón, an impressive archaeological site where Inca engineers took advantage of the natural incline to create a complex hydraulic system composed of fountains, baths, channels and terracing built from finely-carved stone, which served as the setting for different ceremonies or rituals.

San Pedro de Andahuaylillas Located in the province of Quispicanchi, 45 kilometers from Cusco, the "Sistine Chapel of the Americas" is a baroque-style church built in the 16th century over an Inca structure. The interior of this church is decorated with beautiful murals, one of

■ The interior of the church of Andahuaylillas is covered in murals used to evangelize indigenous people.

which dates from 1626. The works of art displayed here —which include murals, paintings and woodcarvings— present a blend of Italian renaissance and Spanish baroque styles. It is interesting to note that some of the phrases visible among the murals are translated into Latin, Aymara and Quechua.

Raqchi Half-way between Cusco and Puno travelers pass the village of Raqchi, where the tallest known Inca structure can be visited. Built during the reigns of Pachacutec and Tupac Yupanqui, Raqchi was a shrine devoted to the worship of Wiracocha, the supreme deity who together with the sun god Inti dominated the Inca pantheon. At Raqchi enormous round columns can be seen, as well as more than a hundred storerooms, or *collcas*, making it unique among the known examples of Tawantinsuyu architecture.

Cusco's Fiestas Emerging from the syncretism of indigenous rites and Spanish Catholicism, Cusco's typical fiestas enable us to participate in the history and living culture of the city. These fiestas are a blend of religious fervor, ancient dances and popular celebration. It is impossible not to be swept along by

■ Enormous mud brick walls with stone bases up to fourteen meters in height are all that remain of the great temple dedicated to the creator god Wiracocha at Raqchi.

■ Every June 24 Inti Raymi, or the fiesta dedicated to the sun god, is staged to recall the most important festival celebrated by the Incas, according to the chronicler Garcilaso de la Vega.

them, for the processions and celebrations take place in Cusco's streets and plazas. The annual festivities include the Festival of the Sun, or Inti Raymi, which is held on June 24 during the winter solstice, and Corpus Christi, which has been celebrated every June since 1572, when it was introduced by Viceroy Toledo as a way of combating native religious worship. In this festivity the images of a number of Catholic saints are carried around Cusco's Plaza de Armas, in the same way that the mummies of Inca sovereigns were paraded in the empire of Tawantinsuyu. During this same month the pilgrimage to Qoylluriti takes place, when thousands of people from all over the southern Andes walk to the snows of the *Apu* Ausangate, at more than 5000 meters above sea level, where they recall the apparition of the Christ Child to a shepherd boy named Manuel in the year 1780.

Right: The *Danzaq* group of dancers at the fiesta of Our Lady of Mount Carmel or "Mamacha Carmen" in Paucartambo. This fiesta of ■ colonial origin is characterized by an abundance of color, music and dance as the feast of the Virgin is celebrated over four days.

The lost city. Machu Picchu is without a doubt the most emblematic and visited place in Peru, as well as an icon of Inca culture, by virtue of its magnificent megalithic architecture and the wild scenery that surrounds it, where the green of the forests combines with the snowy heights of the Andes.

Each year, Machu Picchu is visited by thousands of people who recognize it as one of the greatest wonders created by mankind, as well as sensing the mysterious spiritual halo that surrounds it as they speculate regarding its original purpose.

The majority of the structures which comprise the Historical Sanctuary are framed by the hill known as Huayna Picchu. Construction began under Pachacutec and the city reflects all the typical characteristics of Inca architecture and engineering, which in their turn illustrate the ideology of a people who existed in total harmony with their natural environment, where the divine is present in the everyday.

■ **Above:** The Intihuatana —which means "where the sun is tied"— is perhaps the most emblematic part of Machu Picchu. **Right:** Classic view of the citadel of Machu Picchu, with the *apu* or sacred mountain Huayna Picchu in the background.

■ Agricultural sector with its extensive agricultural terraces.

■ View of the archaeological complex of Machu Picchu from Huayna Picchu, where the entire citadel can be seen, divided into agricultural and urban sectors.

As is well-known, Machu Picchu was mentioned by Augusto Berns in 1867, Charles Wiener in 1870, and Hermann Goering in 1874, but it was Hiram Bingham —with the support of Yale University— who was hailed as its scientific discoverer in 1911.

When walking through Machu Picchu, the visitor is able to identify easily its different sectors. The first is known as the agricultural sector, and it is composed of the terraces and *collcas* located on the slopes that face the Urubamba River. Here, the Incas sowed their crops and stored the harvests that would feed the stable population of the city and be employed for ritual functions, particularly in the case of corn.

The urban sector is located in the upper level, and it is divided by the classic Andean structure of *hanan* (upper) and *hurin* (lower), those complementary opposites. Both of these parts are adjacent to the great plaza, or Chawpi Pata. In the *hanan* zone are located important elements such as the Temple of the Sun, Royal Palace, Temple of the Three Windows, the Intihuatana [or sundial], ceremonial fountains and large *kanchas* [open areas surrounded by several structures]. These and other

buildings are surrounded by a number of towers, storerooms and water channels. In the *hurin* zone, four temples stand out from the other structures: the Temple of the Condor, the Temple of the Mortars, the Temple of the Ceques and Intimachay, or the "Cave of the Sun".

From Machu Picchu one can also see a series of mountains and rocks of colossal size which as well as forming part of the natural setting of the city, were worshiped during the time of Tawantinsuyu as Apus, or the gods of local communities. The Sacred Rock, located in the *hurin* sector, imitates the form of

■ The Tower, or Temple of the Sun, is a unique semicircular structure built over a rock outcrop and displaying fine stonework.

■ Interior of the Great Sacred Cave or Royal Mausoleum beneath the Temple of the Sun.

the nearby hills Yanantín and Puma-sillo, and the most famous mountain in the area, Huayna Picchu, stands as another example of the sacredness of natural phenomena.

Machu Picchu is believed to have been a great palace structure, where administrative and religious functions were inextricably linked.

■ This space was named by Bingham the Temple of the Three Windows, in an allusion to the mythical hill Tamputoco, from where the founders of the empire emerged.

■ The Temple of the Condor. The condor, or *kuntur*, was venerated by the Incas.

■ View of the architecture around the Intihuatana; located at the top of a truncated pyramid, it is believed that it functioned as a kind of sundial.

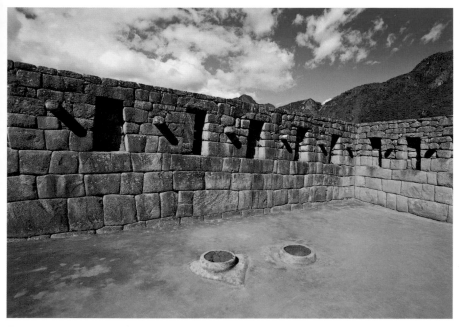

■ The mortars in this sector may have been used for grinding, although some authors believe that they functioned as water mirrors used during astronomical observations.

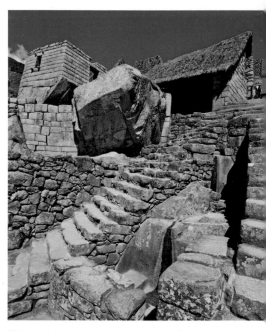

■ Fountains sector composed of sixteen cascades or *pacchas*.

■ The so-called Three Doorways sector is composed of three symmetrical units which probably served as residences for the elite. They are arranged around a *kancha*.

■ The *acllahuasi* housed the virgins devoted to sun worship.

■ One way to reach Machu Picchu is via the Inca Trail, or Capac Ñan.

■ The last section of the Inca Trail leads to the Intipunku, or "Sun Gate", from where hikers are rewarded with a fine view of Machu Picchu.

The Inca Trail to Machu Picchu In addition to observing the megalithic architecture of Machu Picchu, the visitor can enjoy walking the stone pathways that link this marvelous site with the imperial capital. These paths wind sinuously through the green mountains that surround the Historical Sanctuary and form part of an enormous Inca highway system which united all the territories conquered by the armies of Cusco with regional administrative centers and the capital. The highway system ran between southwestern Colombia and northwestern Argentina and is known by its Quechua name, Capac Ñan. This system functioned efficiently because of the *tambos* constructed along its length; structures that served to provide shelter for travelers and facilitated the work of *chasquis*, the messengers at the service of the state who carried vital information between Cusco and the regional capitals by employing a relay system. The Inca Trail that joins Cusco and Machu Picchu can be walked in three days along sections of varying topography and a maximum altitude of over 4000 meters.

Choquequirao Known since the 19th century, the ruins of Choquequirao —"cradle of gold", in Quechua— are in many ways quite similar to those of Machu Picchu. They are located close to the Apurimac River, about three days' walk from the city of Abancay. In what was apparently a religious complex covering around 2000 hectares, different types of public buildings can be observed, but in contrast with Machu Picchu, Choquequirao offers visitors beautiful walls decorated with inlaid images of llamas.

Right: The architecture of Choquequirao —"Cradle of Gold"— is similar to that of Machu Picchu. It was an important political and ■ religious center where the last descendants of the Incas sought refuge for forty years.

Paradise of life and color. The great natural reserve that is the Amazon forest is recognized as the lungs of the planet. These forests cover more than 70% of Peruvian national territory, from the high mountain forest with its rugged topography to the wide, flat expanses of lowland jungle.

Both of these areas are inhabited by typical tropical forest fauna and flora and large areas are protected by national parks, sanctuaries and reserves. Traveling in this region involves the navigating of wide, meandering rivers, including the Amazon itself, the world's most powerful river, as well as the Marañón, Huallaga and Ucayali.

Along the courses of these and many other rivers lie the territories of local ethnic groups such as the Aguaruna and Huambisas in the department of Amazonas, the Ashuar, Urarinas and Cocamas in Loreto, the Shipibos in Ucayali and the Ashaninkas throughout the central forests of Peru. These peoples continue to try to conserve

Above: Hundreds of species of butterflies punctuate the greenery of the jungle. **Right:** With their squawking and colorful plumage macaws bring life and color to the forest that covers 60% of Peru.

■ House of Iron, the city of Iquitos's emblematic building, designed by the famous French architect Gustave Eiffel in 1887, during the rubber boom.

■ Red-headed parrots in the forests of Iquitos.

■ Indigenous people from the Yagua tribe in the outskirts of the city of Iquitos.

their traditional ways of life, in harmony with their natural environment.

Iquitos, capital of the Peruvian Amazon Founded as a Jesuit mission in the 18th century, Iquitos is named after the indigenous people who inhabited the lands around the Amazon River when the Spanish arrived in the region. This city prospered towards the end of the 19th century during the so-called rubber boom, when international demand for this raw material grew on the back of the second Industrial Revolution. Iquitos became the main river port in the jungle and the home of magnates and adventurers who built mansions decorated with beautiful tiles and promenades along the banks of the Amazon. Among the finest examples of this architecture we find the Casa de Fierro ["House of Iron"], designed by Gustave Eiffel, and the old Hotel Palace, which now serves as the local army base.

Pucallpa, red earth Pucallpa, the capital of the department of Ucayali, is the second most important city and port in the Peruvian Amazon region. Here the indigenous culture of the Shipibo people has become fused with the customs brought by colonists who have come from all over Peru since the rubber boom. The city's most important attractions include

■ Typical Yagua hut, built from materials found in the forest. These groups live in small communities on riverbanks in the Amazon basin.

■ House mounted on stilts as a precaution against rising water levels.

■ *Peque peques* are small motorized canoes which are the traditional mode of transport for persons and cargo in Amazon communities. Their name derives from the sound made by the diesel engines.

■ White-fronted capuchin monkeys (*Cebus albifrons*) play among the branches and tops of the trees that form a thick green cover often so dense that rainfall and sunlight do not penetrate as far as the jungle floor.

Lake Yarinacocha and San Francisco Island, where it is possible to stay with indigenous people and also to purchase their beautiful handcrafted pottery and textiles. Another great attraction of Pucallpa is the city's Nature Park, one of the most comprehensive regional zoological parks in the country. Among the species on display, visitors can see anacondas, panthers and pink river dolphins.

Manu National Park, Amazonian paradise Situated in the departments of Cusco and Madre de Dios, Manu National Park covers an area of more than 1,500,000 hectares and is the most

Above: Gray heron flying low over a lake. **Right:** At sundown, the last of the sun's rays are caught by the Amazon vegetation to create ■ a dramatic backdrop just before nightfall.

■ The agouti is a diurnal rodent that lives on fruit and seeds.

■ Black caiman in the forests of Pacaya Samiria, Loreto.

■ Hundreds of species of reptiles and amphibians inhabit the Amazon, including this little nocturnal frog (*Phyllomedusa* sp.).

■ The hoatzin or *shansho* is a prehistoric looking bird.

■ Vast green carpets of flora such as *Victoria regia* cover the waters of the forest lakes, or *cochas*, providing a habitat for insects, small amphibians, reptiles and fish.

important nature reserve in the country. Within its boundaries more than 20,000 species of flora and 3,000 species of fauna are protected, and it is the home of 30 ethnic groups, including the people of the Matsiguenka tribe. Manu National Park has been described as the most biologically diverse area in the world. Several types of forest can be found within the protected area, and its uniquely diverse characteristics make Manu a very special place for those interested in ecotourism, the protection of the environment and the survival of native Amazonian culture.

Tambopata National Reserve This protected natural area is located south of the Madre de Dios River, in the districts of Tambopata and Inambari in the province

■ Curious white-fronted capuchins watch everything that happens below them.

■ The mythology of the Amazon likens the rivers to great serpents, or *yacumamas*, in an allusion to their winding form as they meander through the forests.

of Tambopata, and it covers an area of 278,284 hectares. The great diversity of species that inhabit this reserve makes it a particularly rewarding travel destination. The reserve's *collpas* are places in the forest where huge numbers of macaws, as well as other species including parrots, gather to feed on the minerals they find in clay deposits. In other parts of the forests of Tambopata, visitors may spot large mammals, including tapirs, peccaries and agoutis, as well as roseate spoonbills, jungle condors, harpy eagles and at least 14 species of heron.

■ **Left:** The cock-of-the-rock or *tunqui* (*Rupicola peruviana*) is Peru's national bird. **Above:** *Collpas* are visited each day by macaws and parrots that feed on the minerals essential to their diet. **Right:** Bird watching in Tambopata.

■ **Above:** The Peruvian forest is a universe of colors and textures, a splendid microcosm in which flora and fauna like this heron live in extraordinary harmony. **Right:** Lake Sandoval, situated within the Tambopata National Reserve in Madre de Dios.

■ A group of *Papilio* sp. butterflies gathered in the sand.

■ A cricket (*Orthoptera* sp.) blends in with the dry leaves of the forest.

■ River turtles, known locally as *taricayas*.

Stairway to heaven.

Founded in 1574 as a mining settlement at more than 3000 meters above sea level, the "noble and generous" city of Huaraz is situated in the heart of the Andes, in the Callejón de Huaylas, where Mount Huascarán, the highest peak in Peru, watches impassively over

the lives of those who live at its foot. Huaraz is renowned as a popular destination for those who practice mountain adventure sports. In the area around the city, visitors can enjoy a stunning landscape that offers skiing, rock and ice climbing and trekking. Lovers of mountain life from the Basque country, France, Italy, Switzerland and many other parts of the world have made Huaraz their second home.

But if one thing characterizes Huaraz, apart from its great peaks, it is the fact that its territory is home to one of the most ancient and important temples of pre-Hispanic Peru: the oracle of Chavín de Huántar.

■ **Above:** Stone head of the great temple of Chavín de Huántar. **Right:** Mount Alpamayo rises to 5,947 meters and in 1966 UNESCO declared it the most beautiful mountain in the world.

The monolithic *Lanzón*, the central sculpture of the temple of Chavín de Huántar.

Cupisnique style ceramic depicting an individual cutting their own throat.

Chavín Culture For many years Chavín was considered the first great civilization of the Andes, and it was even described as the first empire. However, in recent years research has established the site of Chavín de Huántar as a place which exerted great influence, in a similar way to the shrine of Pachacámac on the coast south of Lima. The distinguishing features of this megalithic site —representations of hybrid creatures with feline, bird and serpent characteristics— are also found in locations far from Chavín and in different artistic media.

Chavín de Huántar and its Temples The site is located at the confluence of the Mosna and Huacheqsa rivers, at 3185 meters and close to the gateway to the Amazon forest. Construction began around 850 BC and the site was abandoned by 200 BC. The structures that can be seen today are the result of several centuries of continuous construction and remodeling. Two great temples mark the expansion of the site. The Old Temple houses the famous *Lanzón* and the sunken circular plaza decorated with friezes featuring anthropomorphic creatures and zoomorphic motifs; the New Temple is characterized by the Gate of the Falcons and the great square plaza.

The Feline Gods Chavín is remarkable for the artworks produced by its stone carvers, the finest examples of which are the *Lanzón*, the Raimondi Stela, the Tello Obelisk, the tenon heads and the friezes that decorated both the sunken circular plaza and the gateway to the New Temple. These carvings are characterized by their representations of creatures with feline features, fanged mouths and sharp claws. It has been speculated that the figures on the *Lanzón* and Stela were deities who would have been invoked in order to secure a reliable water supply for the society's crops, and that the images on the Tello Obelisk illustrate a mythical coupling that explains the origin of the harvest.

Recuay Culture The Recuay culture emerged in Callejón de Huaylas during the first century AD. It is renowned for its ceramics and monoliths, which show the culture's lords, priests, warriors and shepherds engaged in their everyday activities. The Recuay people occupied a large swathe of the present-day region of Ancash until the Wari expansion (around 750 AD), and the sites of Pashash and Wilcawain contain the most important examples of their architecture.

Recuay craftspeople were expert stone carvers and their public buildings were decorated with great monolithic figures. Unlike the stonework produced at

■ Monochrome, thick-walled and stirrup handled pottery typifies the Chavín style.

■ Recuay culture monolith showing a squatting or praying figure.

■ Recuay architectural ceramic made from white clay, or kaolin.

Chavín, their carvings were made on semicircular stones, many of which are displayed in the grounds of the Ancash Regional Museum. Recuay ceramics combine sculpture and painting, with the upper parts of the vessels adorned with three-dimensional scenes that illustrate aspects of ordinary daily life, while the main bodies are decorated with painted designs.

In both clay and stone, Recuay culture produced many representations of individuals wearing large headdresses and carrying shields, clubs and trophy heads. Further archaeological research will be required to establish if these individuals were associated with actual warfare or with ceremonies involving ritual combat.

■ View of the eastern façade of the temple of Chavín de Huántar. This was an important administrative and religious center and a place of pilgrimage.

■ At 6,768 meters, the southern summit of Mount Huascarán makes it the highest mountain in Peru. At its foot, the village of Yungay was buried by a landslide in 1970 when a section of the mountain collapsed during an earthquake.

Callejón de Huaylas, white mountain peaks The archaeological richness of Ancash is complemented by its impressive landscapes, including that of Callejón de Huaylas, which is framed by the high summits of the Cordillera Blanca and the Cordillera Negra. These beautiful mountainous landscapes with their white peaks and turquoise blue lakes have inspired comparisons with the European Alps, leading to the area being dubbed by some "the Switzerland of Peru", and these mountains provide the setting for the practicing of a number of adventure sports, as well as ecotourism. The Cordillera Blanca is located within Huascarán National Park, which boasts Peru's highest mountains: Mount Huascarán (6768 meters) and Mount Yerupajá (6634 meters). Another special attraction is spectacular Lake Llanganuco, where visitors can enjoy peaceful boat rides, walk around the lakeshore or just contemplate the magnificent scenery. This is a perfect landscape for those who enjoy trekking, and it is inhabited by spectacled bears, pumas, vicuñas and condors, while the native flora includes the remarkable *Puya raimondii* and extensive forests of native *queuña* trees [*Polylepis sp.*].

Right: Lake Cullicocha (4,850 meters above sea level) is located at the foot of Mount Santa Cruz. Its waters form a mirror in which forms, ■ colors and shadows of extraordinary beauty are reflected.

Elegance, mud and *marinera.*

Founded by Diego de Almagro in 1534, from the beginning of its history it was one of the most important cities of colonial Peru, by virtue of its fertile valley and access to the sea. Known as "the city of eternal spring", in recent years it has enjoyed a boom based on

agricultural exports. Recent archaeological discoveries such as the Lady of Cao, and the restoration of the citadel of Chan Chan and Moche pyramids, have attracted thousands of visitors who come to see the impressive vestiges of Moche and Chimu culture. In addition, Trujillo possesses fine colonial and republican buildings in the area around it beautiful main plaza. Bathing resorts like Huanchaco and Las Delicias invite one to plunge into the sea on modern surfboards or ancient reed rafts. Trujillo is also synonymous with good food; its gastronomy is justly famous, with "*ceviche*" and "rice and duck" the most popular dishes.

■ **Above:** Detail from a frieze at Chan Chan. **Right:** In the valleys of Peru's northern coast time seems to have stopped, and on some roads among the cane fields, rice paddies and cotton crops it is common to see peasants using horse drawn carts.

Moche Culture During the first seven centuries after Christ, the Moche culture established a complex culture in which great lords associated with powerful deities ruled a society characterized by its pottery, metalwork, architecture and complex mortuary rituals. Moche society was led by a caste of warriors and priests. They assumed the identities of their principal gods and took part in ceremonies which often involved human sacrifices. This caste controlled an organized mass of workers devoted to the activities that sustained them and provided them with their splendid artifacts.

Pottery and Metalwork In their pottery, the Moche illustrated their worldly and religious lives. Among the globular, stirrup-handled vessels they produced, the "portrait vessels" are particularly interesting; with extraordinary realism they depict the faces of children, young people and the elderly with expressions of mood, distinguishing features and even congenital illnesses. They also produced erotic art —sculptural presentations in clay of sexual scenes— thereby expressing the importance of fertility and associated rites for an agricultural society. Moche ceramists represented intricate scenes of the myths and rites that controlled their world, in black line drawings on a cream background.

Moche metalworkers produced a variety of jewelry and royal emblems used

■ Typical Moche portrait vessel depicting a member of the elite.

■ Erotic vessels are associated with fertility rites.

■ Portrait of the Moche god Ai Apaec carved from wood and inlaid.

■ Headdress with feline head and claws and gold sequins.

■ Chimú wood carving of a priest carrying a ceremonial cup.

■ Sculptural Chimú ceramic depicting a hunter.

■ Monochrome Chimú ceramic decorated with a parrot and its chick.

in life by their rulers in ritual ceremonies, and which in death formed part of their funerary offerings. Created using advanced metalworking techniques, these fine pieces made from gold, silver and alloys were decorated with shell and semiprecious stone appliqués.

Chimú Culture In the 9th century AD, after the decline of the Moche culture as a result of natural phenomena and outside cultural influences, the Chimú kingdom began to emerge, eventually expanding as far as Tumbes in the nor-th and Lima to the south. The legend recorded in the *"Historia Anónima"* (1604) tells of how Tacaynamo was the mythical founder of the dynasty and the first ruler of the capital, Chan Chan.

Ceramics and Metalwork Chimú ceramists tended to use molds and to produce black pottery. Their vessels were mass-produced in workshops at the service of the state. Although their globular form and stirrup handles recall the pottery of the Moche culture, they are inferior in terms of quality and detail. The decoration is simple and leans towards depictions of everyday life and other naturalistic designs, as well as religious themes.

Together with the metalworkers of Sicán, the craftspeople of Chimú are considered the best that the Andean world produced. The Chimú became exceptional metalworkers through their use of the "lost wax" technique, filigree and repoussé, which they employed to produce magnificent works in gold and silver.

■ Mural with mythological scenes, warriors, plants and marine and land animals.

■ Detail of the main frieze of Huaca de la Luna decorated with rhombus-shaped designs and the figure of the principal Moche deity, Ai Apaec, the "decapitator god".

Huaca del Sol and Huaca de la Luna

The archaeological remains of Huaca del Sol and Huaca de la Luna are located in the countryside 5 kilometers south of Trujillo. Surrounded by an urban complex, they were pyramidal and constituted the center of political and religious power in Moche society. Recent work at Huaca de la Luna has revealed bright polychrome reliefs that illustrate parts of the rituals and sacrifices in which gods and rulers interacted.

■ Huaca del Sol, like many Moche pyramids, rises above modern-day fields of crops. An estimated 140 million mud bricks were used in its construction.

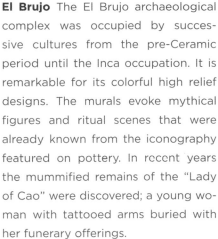

El Brujo The El Brujo archaeological complex was occupied by successive cultures from the pre-Ceramic period until the Inca occupation. It is remarkable for its colorful high relief designs. The murals evoke mythical figures and ritual scenes that were already known from the iconography featured on pottery. In recent years the mummified remains of the "Lady of Cao" were discovered; a young woman with tattooed arms buried with her funerary offerings.

■ The discovery of the Lady of Cao at the main pyramid of the El Brujo complex revealed the role of women in the Moche elite and pre-Columbian power structures.

■ Funerary chamber of the Lady of Cao decorated with polychrome murals featuring interwoven serpents, mythological figures and menacing gods.

■ Naturalistic or stylized marine motifs reflect the Moche relationship with the sea.

■ Detail of the walls and niches of the citadel of Chan Chan.

■ Wall of Huaca del Arco Iris decorated with the figure of a two-headed serpent.

Chan Chan, mud brick city The great Chimú capital is considered the largest mud brick city in the Americas and the second largest in the world after Argé Bam in Irán. Chan Chan —"Sun Sun" in the Chimor language— is composed of the remains of ten great palaces or walled compounds (citadels) that were the homes and subsequently the mausoleums of each of the Chimú kings. They were surrounded by residential neighborhoods and "intermediate" architecture, as well as sunken field systems, or *huachaques*. Chan Chan is remarkable for its beautiful high relief mud decoration, produced using molds, which adorns the walls and is

■ Detail of the entrance of the Main Plaza of the Tschudi Palace (Nik Am), one of the palaces at Chan Chan which served as the home and tomb of a Chimú sovereign.

■ Trujillo's neoclassical main plaza, surrounded by colonial and republican mansions.

■ Window grille typical of the mansions in Trujillo's historic center.

■ Interior of Casa Urquiaga, built in the 16th century. For a time it was the residence of the liberator Simón Bolívar and he organized the liberation campaign from here.

composed of geometric combinations and representations of fish and birds.

The Historic Center Trujillo is characterized by its colonial and republican era buildings, with their wide balconies and stone porticos, conceived in baroque, rococo and neoclassical styles. Many of these houses have conserved their period furnishings. The most notable mansions of the 16th century include Casa Tinoco and Casa Ganoza, while the most emblematic examples of the architecture of the 18th century are Casa Calonge, Casa de la Emancipación and Casa Orbegoso.

■ Huanchaco is a fishing village and a popular resort for the people of Trujillo. Its climate is excellent and its relaxing atmosphere is complemented by the vestiges of a glorious past.

Huanchaco and its sun-gilded reed boats The bathing resort of Huanchaco was an important bay for the ancient Moche and Chimú inhabitants of the area, and a strategic secondary port during the colonial period and the early republican era. Visitors can still observe the totora reed boats known locally as "*caballitos*", which were frequently represented on Moche pottery. These single-person rafts are controlled using a single paddle and are still employed by local fishermen.

The techniques used for making reed boats have been passed on from one generation to the next since the time of the pre-Hispanic ■ Moche and Chimú cultures. Today they are a symbol of Huanchaco's living culture.

Royal tombs and pyramids.

Known as the "capital of friendship" in recognition of the traditional warmth of its inhabitants, Chiclayo is one of the most commercial cities on the Peruvian coast, as a result of its strategic location, which enables it to act as a hub for products that

come from the northern highlands and jungle region. This has also given the city a rich and varied cuisine that is sweetened by desserts made from caramelized milk and crowned by dishes based on fish and rice. It is also home to great archaeological complexes such as Huaca Rajada, Túcume and Batán Grande. In the modern museums of the Lord of Sipán, National Sicán Museum and Brüning Museum, vestiges of Moche and Sicán cultures are displayed. The neoclassical architecture that surrounds the Parque Central includes the cathedral, which dates from 1869, and the Municipal Palace, from the early 20th century. In nearby Lambayeque one finds beautiful colonial and republican mansions.

■ **Above:** Detail of a frieze with crewed reed boats, at Huaca las Balsas, Túcume. **Right:** Sundown over the carob forest. Since time immemorial the carob tree (*Prosopis pallida*) has provided mankind with food, wood and animal feed.

Sicán double neck and bridge handle vessel, painted after firing.

The great Lord of Sicán headdress, found at Huaca Loro.

Representation of a Peruvian hairless dog.

Sicán Culture Sicán —"house or temple of the moon" in the Muchik language— emerged after the decline of Moche culture. According to the legend recorded by the chronicler Cabello de Valboa, its mythical founder, the god Naymlap, arrived on a fleet of rafts from the ocean, founded the dynasty and taught the natives how to work the land and produce artworks. He arrived accompanied by his court and brought with him a green stone idol called Yampallec, from which the present-day name of the department of Lambayeque is derived. During its height, the Sicán culture dominated a large area of the northern coast.

Metalwork Sicán metalworkers produced delicately-finished works of art such as ceremonial masks, vessels, ear ornamentation and the famous *tumis*, or ceremonial knives, employing gold, silver, copper and a number of alloys, decorated with precious and semi-precious stones brought from as far afield as Ecuador and Colombia.

Pottery They produced pieces using molds in tones ranging from black to brown, with globular forms, pedestal bases and double spouts. Under one of the spouts a crowned face with winged eyes was often added, and this feature has been variously identified as the god Naymlap or the Sicán deity.

Economic Activity This people irrigated their desert lands in order to grow a number of crops. The large scale production of metal ceremonial and utilitarian objects was the main economic activity. To this end, they developed an extensive network of maritime and overland trade routes; their ships and merchants traveled as far as the Colombian coast in the north and Chincha to the south, and their products reached the forests and highlands of northern Peru.

Pomac Forest and the Sicán Archaeological Complex The Bosque de Pomac Historical Sanctuary is a reserve created to protect the region's natural and cultural diversity. This dry equatorial forest is home to a wealth of fauna and flora, including carob (*Prosopis pallida*) and sapote (*Capparis angulata*) trees. Mammals, reptiles and more than seventy species of birds inhabit the forest. The archaeological complex is composed of twelve large pyramids which constituted the center of the religious, political and economic power of

■ This ancient, magnificent, twisted carob tree is believed to be about 500 years old and continues to produce fruit.

■ The great pyramids of Sicán rise majestically amid the dense carob forests of the Pomac Sanctuary. Archaeologists have found lavish funerary chambers here with offerings that are now exhibited in the Sicán National Museum.

■ Huaca del Pueblo is one of the pyramids at the mud brick Túcume complex. This site has been eroded over time by wind and rain so that it now resembles a natural landmark.

■ Aerial view of Huaca Larga at the Túcume Archaeological Complex: Here archaeologists have identified three successive occupations: Lambayeque, Chimú and Inca.

Sicán culture. These stepped, truncated pyramids up to thirty meters in height are accessed via a system of zigzagging ramps. When the great lords of this society died, these structures became their mausoleums.

The Valley of the Pyramids: Túcume

Just 33 kilometers from Chiclayo, at the confluence of the Lambayeque and La Leche rivers, is Túcume, the administrative center and capital of the Lambayeque kingdom, composed of twenty-six mud brick pyramids. Huaca Larga is thirty meters high, making it comparable to the structures that travelers might see in the Nile valley or Mesopotamia.

■ Reconstruction of the funerary chamber of the Lord of Sipán; in total eight individuals, a dog and two llamas were interred in order to accompany their master.

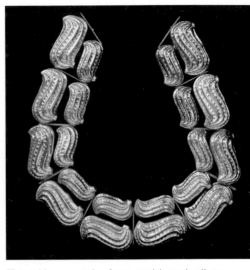

■ Necklace made from gold and silver beads shaped like peanuts.

■ Mask and breastplate shaped like octopus tentacles and made from gilded copper and silver. It formed part of the funerary offerings of the Old Lord of Sipán.

Sipán: Huaca Rajada In 1987 the archaeologist Walter Alva discovered the intact tomb of a great lord from the Moche elite, buried with all the finery that denoted his high status. The discovery became known as the Lord of Sipán, although the foreign press was quick to baptize it as "the Tutankhamun of the Americas". As well as revealing the splendor of Moche culture, the most valuable aspect of this discovery was the information it offered regarding the social organization and ideology of this people, particularly its funerary practices.

The careful preparation of bodies, the special manufacturing of funerary

■ Ear ornamentation of the Lord of Sipán made from gold and turquoise.

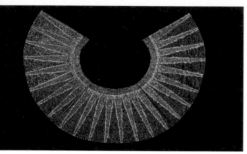

■ Breastplate made from shell beads.

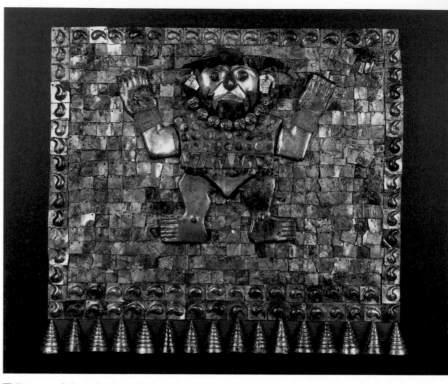

■ Banner of the *Ulluchus* deity, which formed part of the funerary offerings of the Lord of Sipán, decorated with a central figure framed by the enigmatic fruit of the *ulluchu* plant.

wear, the sacrifice of human companions for the journey to the afterlife, as well as animals, provide us with a glimpse of the Moche world view. Ongoing research has revealed the presence of the individual burials of lesser members of the Moche society's elite.

Above: The design of the Royal Tombs of Sipán Museum evokes the pyramidal form of the structures of the Moche culture. **Right:** ■ A reconstruction of the Old Lord of Sipán, dressed in his funerary attire.

Sun and sea.

In the far north of Peru are the regions of Piura and Tumbes, inhabited in ancient times by the Tallán people, the first indigenous group in Peru to experience contact with the Spanish conquistadores, and therefore the oldest mixed race population in Peru.

Piura, land of craftspeople San Miguel de Piura, or San Miguel de Tangarará, was the first city founded by the Spanish upon their arrival in Peru, and since 1532 it has remained the most important city in northern Peru. From Piura, visitors can enjoy the paradisiacal beaches of Colán, Máncora or Cabo Blanco, as well as touring the workshops of the skilled ceramists of the village of Chulucanas, or visiting the expert silversmiths of Catacaos. Not far from Catacaos, one finds the spectacular Narihualá pyramid, a pre-Hispanic mud brick construction that may have been the capital of the Tallán people. Another of Piura's attractions is Huaringas, with its medicinal

■ **Above:** Colán in Piura is one of the most attractive beaches in northern Peru. **Right:** Typical handcrafts from the town of Chulucanas, where traditional pre-Columbian designs are combined with stylized contemporary decoration.

■ The seas of Lobitos beach in Piura are popular with surfers from all over the world, who come to ride the waves and enjoy the tropical climate.

■ Gold and platinum figurine known as the Frías Venus.

■ The craftspeople of Catacaos weave baskets and hats from vegetable fiber.

■ Orange tones shimmer in the idyllic sunset at Colán beach, in Piura.

waters and local healers who call upon natural remedies to ensure the health of their patients.

The prehistory of Piura is represented by the Vicús and Frías cultures. The former was first identified at Vicús hill (located 50 kilometers to the east of Piura), and to date other complexes have been intensively investigated at the sites of Yecalá, Loma Negra and Tamarindo. Vicús craftspeople were particularly skilled metalworkers, fashioning beautiful objects from gold, silver and copper. Although much of their development was contemporary with that of Moche, it would appear that they originated in Ecuador. The Piura Municipal Archaeological Mu-

■ The Cerros de Amotape National Park is a protected natural area that forms part of the equatorial dry forest habitat of mammals, birds, reptiles and amphibians.

■ The comfortable accommodation of the Yemaya Boutique Hotel in Punta Sal.

seum has a large collection of Vicús pieces featuring beautiful examples of the art of this pre-Hispanic people.

Tumbes, sun and sea Occupying the northernmost part of Peru, on the border with Ecuador, Tumbes is a region of unique landscapes that are home to ecosystems ranging from the dry tropical forests of Amotape to the mangroves near the bathing resort of Puerto Pizarro, celebrated for its fishermen and black clam and prawn gatherers. Another local tourist attraction is the Cabeza de Vaca archaeological site, located some 5 kilometers southwest of Tumbes. This was once the seat of the Tallán, culture, before being occupied by the Chimú and, finally, the Incas.

■ The salt water conditions of the Tumbes Mangroves National Sanctuary have created mangroves that are the habitat of birds, reptiles, mollusks and crustaceans.

Between the mountains and the jungle. Founded in 1538 on the banks of the Utcubamba River, Chachapoyas is a beautiful city situated on the rainy eastern slopes of the Andes, within easy reach of the highland

forest and its attractions, including the magnificent Gocta waterfalls, which at 771 meters are the fourth highest in the world. This zone attracts visitors because it was here that the Chachapoyas culture developed, famous for the architectural colossus that is Kuélap, the sarcophagi of Karajía and the mausoleums of Revash and Los Pinchudos, as well as Laguna de los Cóndores (also known as Laguna de las Momias). In recent years more research has been undertaken, and we have learned more regarding the funerary practices of this culture. Two types of burials have been identified: those elaborate sarcophagi placed in caves at the highest part of precipices, and the burial chamber type mau-

■ Above: Detail of one of the circular walls of the citadel of Kuélap. **Right:** Lake of the Condors, where the ancient Chachapoyas people interred the mummies of their rulers in mausoleums located on steep rock faces.

Hypothetical reconstruction of a circular dwelling with a conical roof at Kuélap.

The anthropomorphic sarcophagi or *purunmachus* of Karajía were individual burials in caves carved from steep rock walls.

Another form of interment can be seen at Ravash, where communal mausoleums were employed instead of individual sarcophagi burials.

soleums, also located high up on rock walls. The Leymebamba Museum houses a number of these Chachapoyas mummies and many objects from the different cultures that once occupied the region, including the Incas.

Right: Perimeter walls of Kuélap. Researchers now believe that it was not built as a fortress, but rather as an important administrative ■ center for the production, storage and distribution of food.

		Coastal Andes	High Andes	Coastal Andes	High Andes	Coastal Andes	High Andes	Amazonian Andes	Periods
	World Events	North Coast	Northern Highlands	Central Coast	Central Highlands	South Coast	Southern Highlands	North Central South	

World Events	North Coast	Northern Highlands	Central Coast	Central Highlands	South Coast	Southern Highlands	North Central South	Periods
1600 AD								
1535 AD	Inca 1200 - 1532	Inca 1200 - 1532	Inca 1200 - 1532	Inca 1200 - 1532	Inca 1200 - 1532	Inca 1200 - 1532	Inca 1200 - 1532	Late Horizon 1450 - 1532 AD
1517 AD • Protestant Reformation								
1492 AD • Columbus discovers New World	Chimú 1100 - 1450		Chancay 1200 - 1450					Late Intermediat 900 -1450 AD
	Sicán (Lambayeque) 700 - 1370		Chincha 1200 - 1450				Chachapoyas 600	
1215 AD • Magna Carta signed by King John of England								
1066 AD • Norman conquest of England • Chinese invent gunpowder, 1000 AD								Middle Horizon 600 - 900 AD
800 AD		Cajamarca 200 - 800		Huari 650 - 800		Tiahuanaco 200 - 800		
700 AD								
635 AD • Rise of Arab Empire Mohamed, 570 - 632 AD • Mayan Golden Age	Moche 50 - 800	Recuay 100 - 650						
476 AD • Fall of Rome								Early Intermediat 200 BC – 600 AD
226 AD • Sassanian Empire in Persian								
200 AD						Pucará 200 BC - 200		
44 AD • Assassination of Julius Caesar, 44 BC • Romans conquer Britain, 43 BC	Vicús 200 BC - 200		Lima 200 - 600		Nasca 100 - 700			
0								
140 BC • Venus de Milo					Paracas 700 BC - 100			Early Horizon 900 - 200 BC
200 BC								
326 BC • Alexander the Great conquers Egypt and Western Asia, 336 - 323 BC • Buddha, 565 - 483 BC	Cupisnique 1000 - 200 BC	Chavín de Huántar 1000 - 200 BC						
538 BC • Persia Empire, 538 - 333 BC								
776 BC • First Olympic Games								
875 BC • Age of the Hebrew prophets, 875 - 520 BC								
1000 BC								Initial Period 1800 - 900 BC
2000 BC								
10 000 BC	Hunters							

ANCIENT PERUVIAN CIVILIZATION